Ready to Go → Fundraisers

75 Ways To Fund Your Ministry

07 08 09 10 11 12 13 14 15 16– 10 9 8 7 6 5 4 3 2 1

MANUFACTURED IN THE UNITED STATES OF AMERICA

Development Editor: Josh Tinley
Design Manager: Keely Moore
Production Editor: Susan Heinemann

At the time of publication, all website addresses were correct and operational.

Designer: Keely Moore
Cover Design: Keely Moore

Contents

Contributors

Fundraising ideas contributed by **Lynn Strother Hinkle, Kendra Fredrickson, Theresa Noel,** and **Hannah Plummer;** compiled by **Josh Tinley**

Chapter on writing grants and finding partnerships by **Todd Outcalt**

CD-ROM forms and recipes created and compiled by **Susan Heinemann**

Cover and interior design by **Keely Moore**

Introduction

For many youth ministers, raising funds is part of the job. While their congregations may earmark money in the church budget for youth education and programming, their youth ministry cannot operate on offering-plate money alone. Fundraisers enable youth groups to go on mission trips and pilgrimages, to attend national and regional events, to contribute to worthy causes, and to improve their meeting space.

In addition to bringing in much-needed revenue for your church's youth program, a good fundraiser helps your youth forge relationships with adults in your congregation; and it allows church members to invest their time, talents, and money in the youth ministry. While working together, the students in your group can have fellowship and use their unique gifts and talents for the good of the ministry.

This book provides you with a variety of fundraisers and some tools for pulling them off. Several of the ideas involve hosting dinners or events, great ways to bring your congregation or community together in fellowship. Many activities raise money while providing needed services to church members. The people in your church will gladly support the youth ministry if the teens are willing to watch their kids, wash their cars, or wrap their Christmas presents.

Speaking of Christmas, this book also features several holiday-themed projects, such as selling gifts for Valentine's Day, Mother's Day, and Father's Day; selling lilies for Easter; and helping people clean up the work of Halloween pranksters. Some of the fundraisers involve making goodies or creating keepsakes and require a lot of supplies and preparation. Others are simply creative ways of asking for money that involve little or no start-up costs.

Choosing Fundraisers

Many factors determine how successful any fundraiser is. If most members of your congregation live in the neighborhoods surrounding the church, you can count on people to come out for fundraising events in the evening or on Saturday afternoon. If many members make long commutes, you may need to choose projects that involve selling items after worship or when members are at church for other reasons. If your church has a fully equipped kitchen, you can host a dinner in the building; if not, you may have to rent a facility, use a space in another church, or select another type of fundraiser altogether. If your church already has a tradition of families buying Easter lilies or Christmas poinsettias in honor or in memory of someone, you probably won't want to sell these seasonal flowers to raise money; if not, you have a great opportunity to hold a fundraiser and begin a meaningful tradition. Keep these and other factors in mind as you decide on a way to raise money for your ministry. And remember that no matter what you decide to do, the success of your fundraiser will depend in part on how effectively you get the word out.

Resources Included

This book provides instructions, suggestions, benefits, and lists of supplies for each of the fundraiser ideas. You can find information on safety and sanitation (especially important for fundraisers involving food preparation) on page 105. The accompanying CD-ROM provides additional resources to aid your efforts. If you want to do one of the book's many food sales and dinners, look to the CD-ROM for recipes; if you prefer collecting pledges for an "a-thon," you can print pledge forms from the disc.

Regardless of how you use this book and the CD-ROM, remember that you are raising money for a Christian organization and that your faith must influence every aspect of your fundraising efforts. The following article, "The Precarious Relationship of Money and Ministry," gives you some things to consider as you find ways to generate money for your ministry.

Happy fundraising!

THE PRECARIOUS RELATIONSHIP OF MONEY AND MINISTRY

Jesus famously said, "No one can serve two masters; . . . You cannot serve God and wealth" (**Matthew 6:24**). Throughout history, Christians have struggled with this command. After all, ministry requires money, and church leaders sometimes get carried away (selling indulgences or charging "pew fees" for good seats in the sanctuary, for example). But you have plenty of ways to generate revenue for your ministry without falling into corruption or idolatry.

From the beginning, fundraising should involve prayer and discernment. As soon as you sense that additional revenue is necessary to continue or expand your ministry, go to God in prayer, asking whether you actually need to raise money and what type of fundraiser would be most effective and faithful to your mission. Once your fundraiser is underway, continue in prayer, asking for God's guidance.

Regardless of what sort of fundraiser you do, stay focused on your purpose and remind yourselves and others of why you are raising money. If you are raising money for a mission trip, let people know where you are going and what you will be doing there. If you are generating revenue for a local children's hospital, provide information about the facility; if some representatives of the facility can be present at your event, ask them to attend. If you are raising money to cover operating costs (such as curriculum resources and youth room décor), be up front about what your costs are paying for.

Whatever your aim, let your Christian faith guide you in choosing the fundraiser and the method of carrying it out. Since most Christian bodies oppose gambling, for example, you shouldn't host a casino night or hold a raffle. Christians also profess that the human body is God's temple; thus any meals you serve in conjunction with a fundraiser should be well-balanced and include healthful entrees and sides. Reverence for God's creation means selecting fundraisers that don't involve selling or using disposable items that will soon end up in the trash.

Once the money starts coming in, don't get too caught up in how many dollars you've raised. Instead focus on what that money will be used for. Instead of informing the congregation that you've raised $1000, tell them that you've raised enough revenue to send six students to Appalachia for a mission trip or to send eight pigs to agricultural families in the Dominican Republic through Heifer International. Even if you are just raising money to take your youth to an amusement park, be up front about it and report back on how the students have grown and benefited from this time of rest and recreation.

In a sense, fundraisers are always about money. But when a fundraiser is tied to a ministry, the money has to be secondary to the mission. So as you go about your projects, be clear about your objective and pray "without ceasing" (**1 Thessalonians 5:17**) about how to carry out your fundraiser and how to use the funds you raise.

Writing Grants and Finding Partners

by Todd Outcalt

Money is one of the most common needs of any ministry, and youth ministry is no different. Oftentimes, money (or, more specifically, the lack of it) is what puts a tight grip on ministry, kills a great idea, or puts youth directors in a sleeper hold. Youth ministry deals with tons of financial issues: How can we raise enough cash to take that international mission trip? How can I urge the church board to provide funds for an additional youth ministry staff position? Can we really milk the congregation for another special offering?

Regardless of our approach, many of us youth leaders have often found money to be in short supply. Fundraisers that once raised thousands may now raise only hundreds. Other concerns or needs seem to take precedence over youth ministry and tap into the precious resources of the church. And by the time youth ministry has an opportunity to place financial requests, the church's budget priorities have already been determined.

So how do we raise the money needed? Unfortunately, some methods have become dry and tedious. In many congregations, the same ideas and routines are often revisited year after year as the only source of fundraising: the car wash, the spaghetti dinner, and the "bowl-a-thon." Over time, the fun wears off and the funds dry up.

But what if . . . ?

What if you learned a new and different way to do youth-ministry fundraising?

What if you had a fresh idea that could help raise thousands of dollars for your group?

As you read this book, you'll come across fundraiser ideas that you may never have considered. Give one or both of them a try, and see whether budgeting for your ministry doesn't suddenly become more pleasant.

WRITE A GRANT

Did you know that some people give money away to strangers?

Did you know that some organizations are eager to give money away to youth groups—even yours?

Did you know that your ministry and mission could be underwritten by philanthropic organizations that want to help the church?

Yes, several foundations, endowments, trusts, and other organizations are eagerly awaiting your grant proposal. Many of these organizations exist to help churches, youth groups, other ministries, and non-profit organizations achieve their aims.

If you've never considered writing a grant proposal for your next mission trip or new ministry, don't worry. You're not alone. The vast majority of people in the church never consider foundations or local endowments as a funding source for their needs. Most church leaders consider only the church membership itself as a source of funding.

The from-our-congregation-only approach is shortsighted and shortchanges the church of potential funds that could make a good ministry great or turn a dream program into a real program.

Consider, for example, the following scenario:

> Myra, the youth director, has approached the church council for months, requesting funds to create a new youth space in a nearby barn. Her idea involves creating a stage area for a band, installing a sound system and seating, and furnishing one corner of the barn with couches and chairs that can serve as a place for conversation and snacks. Although the church council likes the idea and sees the need, their response is always the same: no money. After months of hearing this broken-record response, Myra gives up on the vision, becomes disillusioned with church politics and policies, and questions her vocation as a youth minister.

Does this story sound familiar? Many visionaries and dreamers in the church can relate to it.

But dreams can become realities—especially if disillusioned church leaders take the time to write a grant proposal and send it to a foundation that funds religious programs. Grant writing is a way of turning ideas into ministries, and finding the necessary funds to do the work of God. If you are a dreamer and are willing to invest the necessary time and effort, you can write a grant proposal.

Some years ago, I was involved in a grant-writing workshop. I was amazed to discover that well over half the organizations represented were churches. During the event, one woman told our group that her church had just received a grant for a new youth director position. The grant, given by an organization that focuses on local church-staffing needs, enabled the congregation to begin this ministry a year earlier than the congregation had expected—before the church had the money. This grant gave the church a head start on raising money to cover the youth director's salary and benefits in years to come.

This success story is just one among many. But if you are interested in writing a grant for your church, read on.

Step 1: Tell Your Story

You may have never considered writing a grant proposal before. But if you believe that your ministry is important and that you have a vision that is worthy of support, someone involved with a foundation or endowment will likely catch on to your excitement. All you have to do is put your vision on paper.

Begin by carefully crafting a brief history of your ministry. Who are you? What makes you distinct from other churches or ministries in your area? How long have you been in around? What excites you? Where have you come from, and where are you going?

Don't hide your proverbial light under a bushel. Find something about your ministry that is unique and exiting, then tell it. If your youth ministry is in the city, say so. If you are a small group but are doing big things, say what your little group has accomplished. Don't stretch the truth, but carefully consider all of your strengths and celebrate who you are. Help that foundation's board catch the spirit.

Step 2: State the Need

OK, so you need money. Many people do. But no two ministries need money in quite the same way, so you must be specific. Do you need "seed" money to get a new ministry going? Do you need hardware (tables, chairs, equipment, and so on)? Do you need an additional staff person?

For now, just make a list of exactly what you need. Think it through carefully. If you have brand names in mind, write them down. If you wish to hire a particular person, what is her or his name?

Finally, how will receiving this grant meet the need? Will the money help you grow? Will it help you reach out to the community? In what ways? What will your project accomplish? What are your goals? Again, be specific.

Step 3: What's Your Timeline?

When are you going to begin this project? Can you draft a month-by-month timeline for the review committee? When will the project be complete or become self-sufficient? For how long will you need financial support, and how far will the money go?

Step 4: What's Your Budget?

Go back to your list of needs, and place a corresponding financial figure next to it. How much will that air-hockey table cost? How much will that first year's salary be? What about benefits? How much will it cost to take 25 youth 2,000 miles by bus to your mission destination? Include the cost of housing, food, and all other amenities. Then total the items.

Decide whether you will be asking the foundation to cover the entire cost or doing "in-kind" or matching funding. State specifically how much money you are asking the organization to grant you. Regardless of how much you ask for, be up front about your needs and intentions and leave nothing out.

Step 5: Staffing, Reporting, and Accountability

Convincing an organization to grant you money isn't the last step. You have to decide who's going to oversee this grant. You'd be surprised at how many churches get grants that they cannot accept because they haven't asked the questions, Who's in charge of this project? and, Who's going to be responsible for making sure that we use the funds as specified?

Are you going to oversee the project? Is it a group-led effort? Who can sign for the grant according to your church's polity and bylaws?

Who will report back to the foundation regarding how the money was used?

These last two questions are the most important to answer: How will you determine the success of your project? How will you measure results?

Now you are ready to write your proposal. Once you've done your homework and created an outline for your project, you are ready to put pen to paper (or fingertip to keyboard).

Step 6: Submit Your Proposal

By now you are probably wondering, *Where do I send my proposal after I've completed it?* After all, if you don't know a giver, how can you receive the gift?

Don't worry. Hundreds of foundations and endowments exist.

Visit your local library, and swing by the reference section. Here you are bound to find at least a few books listing some of the top foundations in the country or, more importantly, the ones in your home state. If your library doesn't have a foundation reference book, ask your librarian to order one (and many libraries will do so) or request one through interlibrary loan.

You can also find many foundations on the Web. Try *grantstation.com.* This site lists most of the major foundations and endowments that issue grants. You can find more information by checking out the individual foundations' websites. Call or write for submission guidelines or other rules.

Once you have submitted your grant proposal, however, don't just sit around a wait for the dollars to come in. Keep in mind that grants are highly competitive. And while grants can pay big dividends, don't assume that a grant request will magically cover your ministry needs. Keep moving with other income streams. At the same time, make grant writing a part of your annual fundraising efforts.

FIND YOUTH MINISTRY PARTNERS

People tend to give their money, time, and attention to organizations and movements that they consider important. They don't invest in a political party, service organization, or alma mater unless they feel personally invested in it. People who give out of sense of obligation, duty, or sheer habit are few and far between.

Take a few moments to reflect upon your youth ministry. Then ask yourself:

➜ Who are the key players in this ministry?

➜ Who understands my passion?

➜ Who has gifts for and an interest in working with teens?

Pin down the answers to these questions, so that you can generate support (especially financial support) for your youth ministry. And if you do your homework and tell your story well, you'll be surprised at where some of this support might come from.

Some years ago, our church desperately needed a youth-room makeover—not just a new coat of paint or a swatch of second-hand carpet but a substantial renewal. Plans were drawn up, and we brought our vision before the congregation. Naturally, many people wanted to contribute financially to this makeover; but a larger gift was needed to bring it to fruition.

Over the course of two weeks, I entertained several people in the congregation by taking them to dinner and outlining the vision for the new room. At some point during each of these evenings, I asked the person if he or she would consider making a "lead gift," a "special gift," or a "memorial gift" toward this need.

The gift came from a source I had not expected: an aged widow who wanted to make a memorial gift honoring her late husband. Out of gratitude for her gift, we agreed to create a plaque honoring her and her husband that would hang in a prominent place in the youth room.

This special gift enabled us not only to fulfill our vision for this youth space but also to create a future fund for upgrades. And, yes, this widow also became a special friend to the youth, and she was frequently invited to attend youth functions.

When creating youth ministry partnerships, remember that a partner can be anyone who believes in your ministry and identifies with the need or the outreach.

Consider your youth ministry needs, and try one or more of the following partnership ideas:

→ Find partners for a specific mission effort; look for people who are interested or concerned about that particular mission.

→ Find partners who will support your ministry for one to three years. Include these partners in every celebration of your accomplishments.

→ Find partners who will offer special skills (such as carpentry and cooking) that will help offset some out-of-pocket ministry expenses.

THANKING YOUR SUPPORT

Some months ago I attended a stewardship seminar that a university president offered. He wanted to share his insights on fundraising. After all, universities today are able to raise hundreds of thousands of dollars annually (and sometimes hundreds of millions of dollars) from alumni and friends.

One particular tip from this official resonated with me: "Many times, churches fail at fundraising because they fail to thank people for their financial contributions." The man was a faithful member of a local congregation in his town. He confided to our group that in the thirty years he had attended the church and despite the tens of thousands of dollars he had contributed, he had never received a single thank you from any pastor or financial chairperson.

Now, many people will say, "Well, a donor shouldn't need a thank you!" Perhaps this statement is true . . . intellectually. But on an emotional and personal level, it is patently false.

Think about it. Doesn't gratitude inspire us? compel us? stir us? even persuade us to give yet again? Absolutely!

When returning from the seminar, I immediately began a letter-writing campaign, thanking the one hundred largest financial contributors in the congregation. I purchased special stationery, wrote each letter by hand, and wrote something of a personal nature to every family by name.

The results were astounding. Not only did I receive a swarm of letters in return (many affirming the university president's insights, saying, "This is the first thank-you letter I have ever received!"); but I also got notes from people who expressed their appreciation, who opened up and told of some hurt or pain from the past, and who reaffirmed their support of the church.

That simple campaign of letter writing made a big difference in the financial picture of the congregation's ministries and mission. I'm sure that the same would be true for those who support the youth.

If you haven't thanked your contributors, helpers, adult counselors, volunteers, and parents lately, do so as soon as possible. Create an annual dinner for these people, take them to lunch, or write letters.

This simple act will no doubt generate financial support for youth ministry.

And toward that end, ask your church board to make these efforts official by providing the following so that you can say thank you every year:

➔ a small fund for stationery, an annual thank-you dinner for contributors, or both;

➔ a business account so that you can purchase small gifts and tokens of appreciation from time to time or take people to lunch (a fund that will pay for itself ten times over in annual support);

➔ a fund for professionally printed cards or letters that could say thank you and offer an annual outline of your ministry vision, so that your contributors will better understand the spirit and joy of working with teenagers.

These ideas, taken together, will not only provide new ways for raising funds but will also create a new dimension of stewardship in your congregation. Give them a try, and see whether these big ideas don't generate big support.

Fundraisers

ADVENT WREATHS

FAMILY WREATH MAKING

Setting: In your church's fellowship hall or another large space familiar to your congregation, toward the beginning of Advent

Supplies: Grapevine and styrofoam wreath forms, greenery, assorted decorations such as ribbon and pine cones, glue, sturdy metal pins, string or picture-hanging wire

Major expenses: Supplies

Primary source of income: Participation fee or donations

Benefits: Everyone needs a good Christmas wreath to hang on the door, and making one's own Christmas decorations can be satisfying.

Kick off Advent by inviting your congregation to make wreaths. Help promote creativity and togetherness by having families and friends, young and old, work together to make masterpieces for their doors. Publicize the event well, make it festive, and it may become a tradition.

Weeks in advance, get commitments from several church members to bring big sacks full of holly, berries, boxwood clippings, sweet-gum seed balls, pine cones, other types of evergreen clippings, ribbons, bows, and anything else that might go on a wreath.

Have people sign up ahead of time, so that you'll know how many forms wreath forms to buy at your local craft shop. Just to be safe, buy some extras. If you don't have a craft store nearby, consider Michael's (*michaels.com*) and A.C. Moore (*acmoore.com*), which have full online stores. You'll also need sturdy metal pins to attach the greenery to the wreath form. Estimate your cost per wreath. Charge a set amount based on that figure, or let the attendees know the cost and ask for donations.

On the day for wreath making, decide where to lay out the supplies (on tables, a stage, or the floor), keeping in mind persons who cannot bend over to get the materials. Spread out the supplies on sheets of plastic or paper. One eight-foot, rectangular table is space enough for two or three wreaths. Play Christmas music to set a festive mood while the wreath makers work.

Option: Serve snacks or a meal, or combine this fundraiser with Greens and Chili (pages 41–42).

ADVENT WREATHS

Setting: In your church's fellowship hall or another large space familiar to your congregation, toward the beginning of Advent.

Supplies: Wreath forms; cardboard, plywood, or foam disks; five tall candles per wreath form (three purple, one pink, and one white); greenery and assorted decorations such as ribbon and pine cones; glue; candles; sturdy metal pins

Major expenses: Supplies

Primary source of income: Participation fee or donations

Benefits: The chance for households to create centerpieces for Advent devotions

Instead of offering wreaths for the wall or door, help people think about the meaning of the season by inviting them to make Advent wreaths.

Advent wreaths stay inside, where live greenery will dry out quickly; so use plastic or silk greenery. Ask church members and other friends whether they have any artificial greenery they would be willing to donate. Call several discount stores, asking whether they have such décor to donate or sell at a low price.

On the day of wreath making, set up your space in the same manner as in "Family Wreath Making" (pages 21–22). To offer guidance to the participants, distribute copies of "Your Advent Wreath" and "Your Advent Wreath: A Way to Celebrate the Season" (available on the CD-ROM). If you wish to have the first devotion together at this event, make a wreath beforehand and gather everyone around as you light the first candle.

ALL-NATURAL EASTER-EGG HUNT

Setting: On your church grounds or in another outdoor setting familiar to your congregation; on Easter Sunday or the Saturday prior to Easter

Supplies: Eggs, plants and vegetables for dyes, several pots

Major expenses: Eggs, pots, strainer, dye materials

Primary source of income: Ticket sales

Benefit: An all-natural twist to a timeless tradition

If your church hosts an annual Easter-egg hunt (and even if it doesn't), add a new twist to the timeless tradition. Make your egg hunt all natural, with no plastic eggs but just the real thing.

Before having the hunt, decorate the eggs. Use natural plants and vegetables for egg dyes, and consider purchasing free-range chicken eggs. In separate pots of water, boil the following ingredients to create your dyes:

➜ red and yellow dyes: red or yellow onion skins

➜ blue dye: blackberries (which you may need to purchase frozen)

➜ green dye: spinach

➜ pink dye: cranberries or cranberry juice

When the water has reached the desired color, let it cool; then pour the contents of the pot through a strainer. Bring the water back to a boil, and use

it to hard boil the eggs. (Do not to crack the eggs by putting too many in one pot.)

Hide the eggs on your church's property, or arrange to do the egg hunt at a church member's house or nearby park. Make sure that you have enough eggs so that every participant can find at least five or six.

Sell tickets in advance, charge a small entry fee at the event, or simply accept donations. Kick off the egg hunt with a brief devotion, explaining why the egg, as a symbol for new life, is significant for Easter.

A-THONS

A-thons are fundraisers that involve getting donations based on people's ability to do something for a long time or distance. Charity walks and runs often encourage participants to get pledges per mile. Other a-thons have sponsors pledge monetary amounts based on how long a participant can dance or rock in a rocking chair. These fundraisers cost little or no money to set up; and, if the youth group puts enough time and effort into them, they can generate a lot of revenue.

ROCK-A-THON

Setting: A room in your church building, overnight on a Friday or Saturday

Supplies: Copies of a sponsor sheet (on the CD-ROM), rocking chairs, DVDs, CDs, refreshments, sleeping mats or inflatable mattresses

Personnel needed: Several adult volunteers

Major expenses: Any rocking chairs that you need to purchase

Primary source of income: Prepaid donations and pledges

Benefits: Inexpensive setup, a lot of fun

Younger youth, many of whom are getting a taste of independence but still have a bedtime, love an excuse to stay up late. And older youth can always use a safe place to hang out on a Friday or Saturday night. While the teens in this rock-a-thon can relish the chance to get out and stay up late, they will need to stay seated...in a rocking chair.

The rock-a-thon tests how long the youth can rock back and forth in a rocking chair. To pull this off, you'll need one rocking chair for each participant. You'll also need ways to keep the teens entertained and refreshed, such as appropriate DVDs and CDs, snacks, and beverages.

Create sponsor sheets for the rockers, or use the one on the CD-ROM. The sheets should explain that the rockers will attempt to rock in a chair for a total of nine hours—from 8:00 or 9:00 at night until 5:00 or 6:00 in the morning. Give sponsors the choice of making prepaid donations or pledge an amount per hour. You might also ask sponsors to pledge a bonus amount for rockers who go the entire nine hours.

Have adult volunteers work in shifts throughout the night, serving refreshments, popping in movies, and playing music. These volunteers should also watch to make sure that no one stops rocking and to allow for prescheduled stretching and bathroom breaks (such as one per hour). The youth should "rock till they drop"; when they drop, allow them to go to sleep. (Put the boys and girls in separate, chaperoned rooms.)

PAINT-A-THON

Setting: A house or building in need of a paint job; a pleasant Saturday morning, afternoon, or both

Supplies: Plenty of paint, supplies for painting (such as brushes, rollers, and drop cloths), copies of a sponsor sheet (on the CD-ROM)

Major expenses: Paint (unless you can get a paint store to donate to the cause)

Primary source of income: Prepaid donations and pledges

Benefits: Potential for lots of revenue; service to the needy

Like other a-thons, this event involves doing something for a long period of time; but it also provides a needed service.

Select a house or building in need of a paint job, such as a house owned by an older adult or struggling family in your congregation or community. Work with the owner to select a color (or colors) and determine a time to come by and paint. Before buying all of the paint yourself, check with a local paint store to see whether the management would be willing to donate several cans of paint to the cause. Collect painting supplies from families in the congregation. (These items include brushes, drop cloths, masking tape, ladders, rollers, plastic sheets to protect windows, and scrapers.)

Create sponsor sheets for the painters, or use the one on the CD-ROM. These sheets should explain the purpose of the project and the money raised, for how many hours youth will try to paint, and whom the sponsors can contact for more information. Allow the sponsors to pledge a certain amount per hour or to give a prepaid donation.

The longer the youth work, the more money they'll earn and the more good they'll do. But don't let the youth push themselves so hard that their work gets sloppy. They can always come back after the paint-a-thon to finish the job.

Other service-oriented a-thons to consider include clean-a-thons and rake-a-thons.

MOVE-ALONG-A-THON

Setting: An outdoor course a few miles or kilometers long at a time of year when the weather is pleasant

Supplies: Copies of a sponsor sheet (on the CD-ROM), water jugs, small cups, T-shirts (optional), prizes (optional)

Personnel needed: Amateur cheerleading squad

Major expenses: T-shirts (optional)

Primary source of income: Prepaid donations and pledges

Benefits: Inexpensive setup, involvement of the congregation and community

Plenty of fundraisers involve running, walking, or cycling—so why not skipping, scooting, or cart-wheeling? A move-a-thon challenges participants to find a clever way to cover a predetermined distance.

Chart out a course that's a few miles or kilometers long; then start promoting the event. Invite people from the church and community to think of creative ways to get from start to finish; ask these people to solicit pledges and donations. Create your own sponsor sheet for this event, or use the one on the CD-ROM. As an extra incentive, create special T-shirts for the event that will be given out to persons who raise a certain amount of money.

Participants are free to jog or ride a bike, but they'll probably get more donations if they crawl or ride a tricycle. (Running half a mile isn't nearly as impressive as traversing that distance on hands and knees.) To avoid injury, suggest that the movers wear protective gear such as helmets, gloves, and kneepads when they need them.

Provide water at various points along the course, and recruit a local cheerleading squad to root on the movers. Consider awarding prizes for the most creative means of moving along.

FAST-A-THON

Setting: A twenty-four-hour period in your church building

Supplies: Water, juice, Bibles, devotional materials, games, entertainment

Major expenses: None

Primary source of income: Pledges and prepaid donations

Benefits: Important lessons about hunger; introduction to the spiritual practices of self-denial and fasting

The name *fast-a-thon* is a little scary, but rest assured that your teens will not be starving themselves. Rather, they will be raising awareness about world hunger and bringing in funds for your ministry. Schedule a twenty-four-hour period during which your youth are locked in the church building without food. Allow them to consume only water and juice during this time. Obtain permission forms for all youth, and instruct them to eat full, balanced meals (and not to skip any meals) on the days before the fast.

In the weeks leading up to the fast, have the youth solicit donations from sponsors. For this fundraiser do not take pledges, because the youth may feel pressured to fast longer than they are capable of going without food.

Play games that aren't physically taxing, and watch movies to keep the teens' minds off their hunger. (See the licensing note on the CD-ROM.) Periodically, give the youth a chance to write in a journal about their experience. Also, use this experience as an opportunity to talk about hunger in the world and in your city, Jesus' fasting in the wilderness (**Matthew 4:1-11; Luke 4:1-13**), and the spiritual disciplines of fasting and self-denial. (For more information on teaching these practices, read *Soul Tending: Life Forming Practices for Older Youth and Young Adults* [Abingdon Press, 2002].)

If at any point a participant feels that he or she cannot go any longer, allow the youth to bow out and contact his or her parents. Don't force the participants to fast any longer than they feel they can.

Afterward, talk about the experience. What did the youth learn about hunger and how it affects a person physically, mentally, and emotionally? Did they feel hunger pains or get irritable? Did fasting give them a sense of satisfaction and accomplishment?

BAKE SALE

Many people are born with a sweet tooth. Thus, a market for home-baked goodies will always exist. The old, standard bake sale can sweeten your youth ministry's treasury and provide a lot of fun. Of course, you'll need to plan ahead, particularly in the areas of advertising, baking, and selling.

Setting: A weekend afternoon at a location familiar to most people in your community

Supplies: Several baked goods (some made by youth, some made by others in the congregation and community), promotional materials

Expertise needed: Price knowledge of a few people who are familiar with prices of baked goods

Major expenses: Ingredients for any baked goods prepared by the youth

Primary source of income: Sale of baked goods

Benefits: Low overhead cost, involvement of congregation members and community, easy setup

Advertising: At least three weeks before the event, put notices in the church newsletter, on the church website, and in the bulletins. Contact area daily and weekly newspapers about placing ads or notices, and provide announcements for local radio stations. Many grocery stores and drug stores have community bulletin boards on which you can hang fliers and posters. You might also ask some local businesses for permission to put posters in their windows.

Any notices should include the time and location of the event, the name of your group, and the cause for which the money will be used (such as a mission project, ski trip, or choir tour). If your group is well known for making a special item (such as pecan fudge), mention it prominently in your ad.

Baking: Each youth may choose to bake an item at home and bring it to the sale. Or the group may choose to work together on a pie, pastry, or other recipe that your group is known for. Or do both, if you wish.

If your students bake individually, ask them what they will bring so that you can advertise those items. Persuade a few local celebrities (such as the mayor, a high school basketball coach, a radio DJ, and the baker who makes the world's greatest cream pies) to donate their baked goods to your sale. Make sure that you sale offers an abundance of items.

Important: *Follow the Safety and Sanitation Guidelines on page 105.*

Selling: Secure the location of your sale well in advance. In county-seat towns, a courthouse square is often popular. In other communities, a mall or other shopping area might work. Many large cities have pedestrian-friendly districts that may offer a good setting for your sale. Remember that you and your group are the guests of those who allow you to use their space; respect their guidelines, and try not to interfere with their regular business.

Some group members should arrive early on the day of the sale to set up tables. Ask one or two people who are familiar with prices of baked goods (such as adults from your congregation) to mark the price of each sale item. Have with you small bills and coins equal to about one-fourth the total value of the baked goods you have for sale. Assign specific times to persons who will be selling the goodies. Having a good time at your sale is important; fun is as much a reason for a bake sale as money. But don't have so much fun that you forget your customers.

BREAD FOR THE FEAST

Setting: Your church kitchen or the home of one of your youth (for baking the bread), before and after worship and church activities the Sunday or Wednesday prior to Thanksgiving (for selling the bread)

Note: If you make the bread more than two days before Thanksgiving, you may need to keep it frozen then let it thaw shortly before the sale.

Supplies: Items for bread making (listed below), plastic bags for packaging

Major costs: Ingredients for the bread

Primary source of income: Bread sales

Benefits: The chance to offer bread to round out Thanksgiving meals and to teach the youth a valuable skill

Before you bake the bread, set aside a block of time (depending on the kind of bread the group chooses) for baking and packaging. This period might encompass a whole afternoon or an afternoon and evening.

Gather these supplies: bread pans, baking spray or butter, flour, and plastic bags for packaging. Decide whether to use bread dough, bread mixes, or ingredients for making bread from scratch. You can buy bread dough freshly made from a bakery, or look for the frozen kind at a grocery store. If you opt for bread mixes, you also will need eggs, water, oil, and any other ingredients listed on the package.

Begin advertising the bread sale two or three weeks prior to Thanksgiving, so that people can plan to buy bread for the holiday at church. Sell the bread before and after worship and church activities on the Sunday and Wednesday before Thanksgiving. You might offer samples to people attending Sunday worship. Determine a price for your bread by looking at the prices for fresh-baked bread at local bakeries and grocers.

THANKSGIVING BAKE SALE

Setting: At your church, the weekend or Wednesday prior to Thanksgiving

Supplies: Baked goods provided by your youth and their families

Major expenses: None

Primary source of income: Sales of baked goods

Benefits: Inexpensive setup, the chance to give people something to bring for Thanksgiving dinner

Sure, bake sales are a dime-a-baker's-dozen. But at Thanksgiving, many people are expected to bring a dish to the family gathering, regardless of their culinary ability or amount of spare time. By selling fresh-baked, ready-to-go delicacies for Thanksgiving dinner, you can save folks a lot of headaches. Have your bake sale the weekend before Thanksgiving or on the Wednesday prior to the holiday, and make your event festive.

Each youth (with his or her family) can sign up to bring a cake, cookies, bread, or pie decorated for the holiday. Examples of appropriate items include pumpkin pie, pumpkin bread, cupcakes with candy pumpkins or pilgrim or turkey picks on them. Encourage the participants to be creative.

Announce the bake sale two or three weeks in advance, so that people can plan to buy their holiday desserts at church. Emphasize in your promotions that many of the items for sale will have a distinctive, Thanksgiving theme.

BIRTHDAY CALENDARS

Setting: Throughout the autumn at your church building

Needs: List of church members' birthdays, pictures of church members, and contact information for a print shop that will print calendars

Major expenses: Printing

Primary source of income: Calendar sales

Benefits: Meeting a need, helping strengthen relationships in your congregation

Many churchgoers would love to have a calendar that tells the birthday of every congregation member. This way, they would be more able to call or send cards to one another on their birthdays and would grow closer as a community.

Call several printing companies or office-supply stores with copy shops, and find one that makes professional-looking calendars for a reasonable rate. You can design the calendars yourself by putting a couple of computer-savvy youth in charge of this task; or turn over some pictures, a list of birthdays, and some basic instructions to the printer and let this company do the rest.

Begin the project in August if you can. You'll have the most success by selling calendars in November or early December. Publicize your calendar sale in October or early November, before people buy their calendars for the coming year.

READY-TO-GO FUNDRAISERS

BOOK, CD, AND DVD SALE

Setting: A Saturday in a large space in your church building or elsewhere in your community

Supplies: Lots of donated books, CDs, and DVDs; promotional materials; price labels or signs; tables; cash box (such as a shoe box); loose change and bills; permanent markers (optional)

Major expenses: None

Primary source of income: Sales of books, CDs, and DVDs

Benefits: No start-up costs; waste reduction by giving new life to used items

Look through your CD collection. How many of the albums on your shelves do you still listen to? How many haven't been touched in five years? Now glance through your DVDs and old videocassettes. How many of these movies have you watched in the past year? How many have you watched only once? OK, now take a look at your book library. Have you read all of these books? Do you plan to? Of those you have read, how many will you read again?

Once you've answered these questions for yourself, ask them of your congregation. Chances are that your church is full of forgotten albums, books, and movies that could find new life in the home of another owner. This library of castoffs can also generate funds for your ministry.

Set a date for your yard sale, and solicit items well in advance. In addition to books, albums, and movies, consider including items such as video games and T-shirts.

Check each item to make sure that its content is appropriate for a church fundraiser. (For example, avoid selling objectionable movies, albums with advisory labels, and M-rated video games.) Promote your sale in your congregation and throughout your community. You might post fliers on grocery-store bulletin boards or put a notice in a local or neighborhood newspaper. Send a notice to websites that cover local happenings.

A day or two before the sale, head to the bank and obtain plenty of nickels, dimes, quarters, and dollar bills. Assign someone to be the cashier, and give this person the cash box.

When you set up the sale, organize the items by type (books, CDs, and so on) and genre (fiction and nonfiction, drama and comedy, country and rap, and so on). Since you won't have to invest in any of your merchandise, you can sell books, CDs, and DVDs at low prices. A good rule is to charge about 10 percent of the original retail price for CDs, DVDs, and newer books; charge a lower price for older books. Mark the prices with labels that you print up on a computer or write on with a black marker. If possible, purchase labels that can be removed without harming the surface of the item they're affixed to. Or, instead of using price labels, assign a price for all the items in a merchandise category and put up signs that say what the prices are.

The items that don't sell can be kept for a future sale or donated to a thrift store or local mission.

CANDLES FOR SAINTS

Setting: At your church building, before and after the All Saints Day service

Supplies: Materials for making candles, food for a dinner prior to the All Saints Day service

Major expenses: Candles or materials for candle making plus the Candle Making handout (on the CD-ROM), food, candle holder, matches or lighter

Primary source of income: Candle sales

Benefits: Keeping alive the memory of saints who have died

This fundraiser is to be held on All Saints Day, in memory of loved ones who have died. The event involves a dinner prior to your congregation's All Saints Day service and a brief but meaningful ceremony of lights right after the service.

The dinner should be something easy to manage, such as spaghetti or soup and salad. The service should be simple; work with church leaders to develop it. To find appropriate poems, songs, readings, and prayers for your program, use official materials from your congregation or denomination (such as hymnals, worship books, or official websites).

Advertise weeks before the occasion, especially if an All Saints Day service isn't an established tradition in your church. In your promotion, invite church members to order candles in memory of loved ones who have died. Purchase some candles, or buy the necessary materials for candle making and follow the directions on the Candle Making handout (on the CD-ROM). Make enough candles to cover all of the orders, plus several extras.

On All Saints Day, arrange the candles attractively on a table; put one of the extras in a candle holder in the center. After dinner, if you have enough space, gather everyone in a large circle around that table. Begin the ceremony of lights by illuminating the center candle. During the service, call forward, one at a time, those who have purchased candles. Invite each of these people to say the name of the person he or she is remembering, make any remarks about this special person, and reverently light the candle. When that participant returns to the circle, call the next person forward. After all of the candles are lighted, read a concluding poem or sing a concluding hymn. Allow the persons who purchased candles to take their candles with them.

CANDY SALE

Setting: Your church kitchen or the kitchen of a family involved in your youth ministry

Supplies: Ingredients, candy recipes (on the CD-ROM), boxes or bags for the candy

Major expenses: Ingredients

Primary source of income: Candy sales (by the box or the dozen)

Benefits: Youth learning the skill of candy making; the potential to bring in a lot of money

Many church and school groups sell candy to raise money. But too often, the candy they sell is the same candy you can buy at any gas station. This fundraiser involves candy that is more difficult to find: homemade candy.

First you will need to decide what candy (or candies) you will make and sell. Here are some possibilities:

➜ peanut brittle, a hard candy made from peanuts and syrup;

➜ candied pretzel sticks, which are dipped in vanilla coating;

➜ lemon crunch, creamy bark with bits of hard lemon candy;

➜ orange-cappuccino cream cups, pastries with chocolate-coffee filling;

➜ buckeyes, balls of peanut butter coated in chocolate;

➜ fudge squares, a creamy chocolate blend with walnuts;

➜ turtles, pecans covered in chocolate and caramel;

➜ Viennese coffee balls, which are powdered with sugar;

➜ peppermint bark, crushed peppermint candies mixed with white chocolate.

If you know of an experienced candy maker from your congregation or community, enlist this person to teach the youth the finer points of confection making. Set a price per box or per dozen. Aim at making plenty of sweets; you'll find ways to sell them once they're made. Most candies are inexpensive to make and use ingredients that can be bought in large quantities.

Package the candies in attractive small bags or boxes, and sell them after Sunday school or worship on Sunday.

CAR WASH

Setting: A Saturday morning or afternoon in a high-traffic area where water and electricity are accessible

Supplies: Rags, at least one water hose, brushes for cleaning tires, detergent, towels, buckets, glass cleaner, vacuum cleaners, a large sign, marker

Personnel needed: Adult volunteers

Major expenses: Any supplies that cannot be provided by the participants or donated by members of the congregation

Primary source of income: Donations

Benefit: Providing a valuable (and needed) service

To attract customers to this tried-and-true fundraiser, make it "free"—that is, charge nothing for the service but accept donations. Some people may take advantage of the free offer without donating; but when you clearly advertise the cause to which the money will go, this method can generate more revenue than sales from a set amount for tickets or services.

When preparing for the car wash:

→ choose a location that has a plentiful water supply.

→ gather plenty of supplies (such as a water hose, buckets, rags, brushes for cleaning tires, detergent, sponges, towels, and glass cleaner).

→ get two vacuum cleaners, so that two people can vacuum the inside of a car simultaneously (one on each side). Vacuum the cars away from the wash area to avoid wetting the interiors and the vacuum cleaners. Instead of letting the teens move the cars from the vacuum cleaners to the wash area, let the car owners do so. (One dented fender will wipe out your profits, cause an insurance nightmare, and do little for public relations.)

→ take long outdoor extension cords if electrical outlets are not conveniently located.

→ get as many youth (and adult volunteers) involved as possible, so that you can work quickly and wash lots of cars. If you have enough help, you can wash and vacuum multiple cars at once.

→ advertise by making a large sign that passersby can see.

→ plan to return all borrowed equipment and supplies promptly and to leave the car-wash area clean and orderly.

CELEBRITY LOOK-ALIKE CONTEST

Setting: An evening in your church's fellowship hall or at another location familiar to many in your congregation and community

Supplies: Food, beverages, napkins, cups, any necessary plates and utensils, a microphone and PA system

Personnel needed: Contestants and judges

Major expenses: Food and beverages

Primary source of income: Admission sales

Benefits: Fun for the entire congregation; bringing out a different side in people

To let your church members let their hair down and have fun, hold a celebrity look-alike contest. Beforehand, ask certain people in your congregation to take part in the contest. Open the event to children, youth, and adults.

Contestants can imitate well-known persons, such as TV characters, athletes, politicians, a youth worker, or another church leader. (The only restriction is that all impersonations should be presented tastefully and without degrading the person being imitated.) Instruct the contestants to look the part and prepare a talk or musical number to be delivered in character.

Consider setting a time limit on each act, and organize the presentations by time slots beforehand. You might also have an announcer ask each look-alike a few questions about his or her character.

Select a panel of impartial judges, as well as categories such as "most authentic," "most original," "most creative," and "best of show." Award a ribbon or certificate for the winner of each category.

Boost profits and promote fellowship by selling refreshments or having a simple meal at the event.

CHILDREN'S STORYBOOKS

Setting: Several weeks of story compilation, culminating in a story hour one afternoon or evening at your church

Major expenses: Book duplication and binding

Personnel needed: Children with stories to tell, an adult to read stories, youth with computer skills

Primary source of income: Sales of books

Benefits: Giving children a voice, giving youth an opportunity to better get to know the children in the congregation

Most young children enjoy hearing stories; even more, they enjoy listening to their own stories. This fundraiser involves a compilation of stories told or written by the children of your congregation.

Arrange with parents of young children in your church to set up times for youth to interview the children and get their stories about various subjects. After recording the stories, the youth can type them up and put them together in a book that you can reproduce for the entire congregation. You might select a theme for your book of stories and focus on a specific time of year, such as Christmas, Easter, or summertime or on other topics such as hobbies and favorites.

Invite older children to submit stories or poems they have written. Ask all of the children who contribute—both those whose stories you record and those who submit their own—to draw illustrations to go with their work.

Enlist youth with computer and artistic skills to put the stories and illustrations together. Print and copy the pages, and have the books bound at a copy shop.

Plan a children's story hour to promote and sell the books. During this time, give any child who contributed to the book a chance to read or tell his or her story. Children who are too shy to read their stories aloud may ask an adult to read for them.

Print some extra copies of these books, and donate them to local school libraries and the children's wings of nearby hospitals.

CHILI SUPPER

CHILI SUPPER

Setting: A winter evening in your church's fellowship hall or another space familiar to your congregation

Supplies: Promotional materials, chili ingredients, cold beverages, cups, bowls, plates, napkins, dining utensils, crackers, toppings such as onions and shredded cheese, condiments such as sour cream and hot sauce, side dishes such as cold salads and cornbread

Major expenses: Chili ingredients

Primary source of income: Ticket sales or donations

Benefit: Providing a hot meal when the weather's cold

Select a cold winter evening, and give the members of your congregation a choice: chilly, or chili? A lot of them will choose the latter.

Get a good chili recipe (or two or three) from a member of your congregation, or choose from the recipes included on the CD-ROM. In addition to a warm pot of spicy, meaty chili, consider providing mild, low-fat, and vegetarian options. Of course, the type of chili and sides will depend on the tastes of your congregation and in what part of the country you reside.

In your promotional materials, use the cold weather to your advantage. Sell tickets in advance to get an idea of how many people you'll be serving, or accept donations at the door. Also, consider working with a ministry in your community that serves homeless or hungry persons and inviting some people who will truly appreciate the hot meal.

CHILI COOK-OFF

Setting: An evening or weekday afternoon

Supplies: Several pots of chili prepared by church members or others in the community, beverages, cups, bowls, napkins, dining utensils, crackers, toppings such as onions and shredded cheese, condiments such as sour cream and hot sauce, dessert (optional), promotional materials, award certificates

Major expenses: None

Primary source of income: Cost of admission (either a set price or donation)

Benefits: Low overhead, involvement of church and community, easy setup

When the weather gets cold, help your congregation and community stay warm—hold a cook-off! The cooks won't have to shell out much money, and your profit margin will be high. Pick a convenient time for the fundraiser, such as before an evening program on a frosty night or after church on Sunday.

Get as many people as you can to submit a big pot of their own chili. Recruit volunteers to serve as judges, and determine a handful of categories for judging, such as "Most Likely to Please Your Mother," "Spiciest," "Most Original," and "Best Overall." Find someone who can be enthusiastic about the contest to be an announcer. Ask youth who are computer savvy and artistically inclined to create award certificates for each of the categories.

GREENS AND CHILI

Setting: In your church building on an evening around the beginning of Advent

Supplies: All of your church's usual Christmas decorations, a tried-and-true chili recipe, as well as these things to eat:

→ chili ingredients
→ crackers
→ cheese
→ onions
→ hot sauce and other condiments
→ desserts (such as ice cream or a sundae bar)
→ cold salads (such as green gelatin salad and Waldorf salad)

And don't forget beverages, napkins, bowls, plates, cups or glasses, and silverware. You might also provide a meatless chili for vegetarians and attendees who would prefer a low-fat option. (See the CD-ROM for a vegetarian-chili recipe.)

Personnel needed: A few adult volunteers

Major expenses: Food and supplies for place settings

Primary source of income: Dinner donations

Benefit: Introduction to a meaningful tradition (hanging of the greens) or one more reason (chili) to look forward to the occasion

Spice up your church's hanging of the greens with this fundraiser.

Invite the congregation to join in a fellowship meal and worship service of hymns and Scripture readings, along with helping decorate the church for the Advent and Christmas seasons. Ask your pastoral staff or the worship committee for guidance in planning the evening.

You can't charge people to participate in the hanging of the greens; the fundraiser is a chili supper in conjunction with the event. Gather the youth in the church kitchen, and prepare the meal together. Or make assignments and have the youth and adult volunteers prepare the food at an earlier time. You can transport the chili to the church in several electric cookers. Instead of charging a flat fee for the dinner, ask for donations. No one will be left out for lack of money, and some people will donate extra amounts.

Option: Combine this fundraiser with the "Chili Cook-off" on page 41 or the "Heavenly Sundae" fundraiser on page 72.

CHOCOLATE FAIR

Setting: Evening or weekend afternoon at your church building or a location familiar to most people in your community

Supplies: Several chocolate dishes (prepared by church and community members); tables and chairs; plates; utensils; cups; beverages such as water, milk, and coffee; tickets; promotional materials

Major expenses: Plates, cups, and utensils

Primary source of income: Selling tickets

Benefits: Low overhead cost, sale of products that easily sell themselves

What better idea for raising funds than chocolate pie, chocolate ice cream, chocolate cookies, and everything else chocolate?

Several weeks before the chocolate fair, nail down the date, location, and time. Ask "chocolateers" (chocolate lovers) to make their favorite chocolate dishes and bring these confections to the event.

Find a location with ample space. In an inner circle, place several tables and chairs for guests. Have the chocolate booths in a larger outer circle.

For weeks leading up to the fair, advertise in newspapers, put a notice on your church and youth ministry's website, make posters, and sell tickets. (Consider setting up a PayPal account, so that you can sell tickets online.) Let the public know that their ticket will entitle them to taste all of the chocolate treats.

When the volunteers arrive with their dishes, make a label for each dish. Ask two people to serve at each station. Make sure that plenty of plates, spoons, forks, napkins, cups, beverages, and wet towels are available.

As guests enter, hand them menus that include the floor plan. To make the occasion more festive, arrange for live entertainment or recorded music.

Stay open as long as the customers wish, and let them enjoy the sweet treats.

COFFEE TREATS

Setting: Before and after worship services and Sunday school, or whenever coffee is served

Supplies: Doughnuts, bagels, sweet rolls, other baked goods, appropriate condiments (such as cream cheese)

Major expenses: Cost of the baked goods

Primary source of income: Sale of baked goods

Benefits: Ready-made customer base, low overhead cost, appeal to late sleepers who skip breakfast to get to church on time

Many church communities are as likely to serve coffee as they are to serve Holy Communion. If the members of your congregation enjoy drinking coffee before church, after church, or between worship and Sunday school, you have an excellent opportunity to create an ongoing revenue stream.

Ask your church's administration for permission to sell doughnuts and bagels on Sunday mornings. Poll the adult classes to see how many bagels, doughnuts, bear claws, or other breakfast goodies you might sell on a given Sunday. Make arrangements with a bakery to have the items ready for you early Sunday morning. Ask about day-old breads and pastries for a reduced price.

If by chance your church does not serve coffee, inquire about interest in beverages. Consider providing juice, coffee, and tea. (Keep in mind that some adult classes prefer to make their own coffee.)

Assign at least one person to pick up the food and juice. If your group decides to offer coffee, recruit several youth to make it and handle the

selling. Make sure that your sale does not interfere with worship. Finish selling and cleaning up in time to get to the service.

COOKIE SALE

Selling cookies isn't terribly creative; but as the Girl Scouts have shown us year after year, it can be effective.

Cookies aren't exactly expensive or difficult to find. But homemade cookies, baked from scratch, can be hard to come by, especially for families who don't have the time or knowledge to make them. By taking the initiative to tear open some bags of flour, crack some eggs, and break out the rolling pin, you and your youth can give members of your congregation the experience of biting into a homemade cookie.

You can sell small cookies by the pound, medium-size cookies by the dozen, and giant cookies one at a time. Ask members of your church to contribute their cookie recipes and help bake. You can also find cookie recipes on the CD-ROM or by clicking the weblinks on the CD-ROM. Check the prices at local bakeries and grocery stores to determine a reasonable price.

To increase profit, make the packaging attractive. You might put some cookies in a clean, inexpensive glass jar and tie some ribbon around it.

CHRISTMAS COOKIES

Setting: In the kitchen and before and after worship and Sunday school on the Sundays leading up the Christmas

Supplies: Decorative boxes or jars, bags, ribbons, and wrappers; small cards or slips of paper with an inspirational message; recipes (on the CD-ROM)

Personnel needed: Volunteers to bake cookies

Major expenses: Ingredients for cookies (unless volunteers pay for them)

Primary source of income: Cookie sales

Benefit: Giving busy families a chance to enjoy homemade Christmas cookies

For many families, the Christmas season just isn't complete without homemade, holiday-themed cookies. Of course, for many families, the Christmas season is so loaded with church activities, shopping, final exams, school plays and concerts, athletic events, and family gatherings that finding the time to bake cookies is nearly impossible. So your youth group has a perfect opportunity to give people a tasty respite from the restlessness that each December brings.

Make a list of varieties of Christmas cookies to sell. (Examples include gingerbread cookies and iced sugar cookies shaped as stars and Christmas trees). The CD-ROM has links to websites where you can get more ideas.

Invite families of youth and other volunteers from your church to sign up to bake a certain number or a certain type of cookie. (For example, the Jones family might sign up to bake four dozen angel-crisp cookies.) If not enough volunteers are available to bake some cookies, find a weekend afternoon in early December to gather at the church kitchen or the home of one of your youth group families to bake several dozen cookies. If you do your baking several weeks before the sale, freeze the cookies.

Sell your cookies by the pound, by the dozen, or individually before and after worship and Sunday school on last few Sundays of Advent. Put the cookies in decorative boxes or bags or jars or wrap them in clear, red, or green plastic wrap. Attach a small card or slip of paper to each item, featuring a short message that emphasizes the true meaning of the season. (A Christmas Bible verse such as **Luke 2:14** would be appropriate.)

VALENTINE COOKIES

Setting: Before and after worship and Sunday school for several weeks leading up to Valentine's Day, plus one afternoon prior to the Sunday before Valentine's Day in your church kitchen or at someone's house

Supplies: Ingredients and supplies for baking and decorating cookies, heart-shaped cookie cutters, plastic bags for holding cookies, tape, order forms, adhesive tape, heart-shaped pieces of paper, recipe (on the CD-ROM)

Major expenses: Cookie ingredients and decorations

Primary source of income: Fee for ordering Valentine cookies and having them delivered

Benefits: Giving members of the congregation an easy way to express love and appreciation

Offer a special way for parents to send messages to their children, friends to their friends, children to their parents or grandparents, spouses to their spouses, and church members to their pastors or Sunday school teachers. Before and after worship and Sunday school, for several Sundays leading up to Valentine's Day, take orders from folks who want to send Valentine cookies to a special someone. Offer several choices of messages for the cookies (such as "I Love You," "Thanks," and "Be Mine").

Give your customers pieces of red, pink, and white paper that are cut into the shape of a heart, and allow them to write personal messages to their Valentines.

For the baking and decorating, schedule a day before the Sunday the cookies are to be delivered. Bake using a basic sugar-dough recipe. (One is provided in the CD-ROM.) With four- to five-inch-wide cookie cutters, cut the cookies into heart shapes. Bake them, let them cool, and decorate them with the appropriate messages. Allow the icing to dry. (If you plan to make the cookies several days in advance, freeze them and allow enough time for thawing.)

After the frosting is dry, place each cookie in a plastic bag. When the delivery day arrives, tape the personal notes with tape to the outside of the bag and make the rounds.

OTHER-HANDED COOKIE SALE

Setting: Before and after worship and Sunday school

Supplies: Several batches of cookies that the youth prepare using only their non-dominant hand

Major expenses: Ingredients for the cookies

Primary source of income: Cookie sales

Benefits: Ready-made customer base, a lot of fun to prepare

Conduct this cookie sale as you would any other cookie sale, with one exception: Have right-handed teens use only their left hand when they make the cookies, and left-handers only their right hand. If a student faces a two-handed task, such as opening a bag of chocolate chips, have him or her ask for help. These cookies should taste the same as your normal homemade cookies.

When the youth have finished baking, have them bag the cookies and hand them to customers in the same other-handed manner.

CREPE DINNER

What is a crepe?

A crepe is a thin pancake made of flour; other ingredients include eggs, milk, butter, and a pinch of salt. Crepes originated in France and are popular throughout Europe. Their fillings can include meats, cheese, vegetables, fruits, and nuts. They can be rolled or folded and topped with any variety of toppings.

Setting: Evening in your church's fellowship hall or an area banquet hall

Supplies: Ingredients for crepes and side items; crepe pans; fine china, crystal, and silverware; card tables; tablecloths; candles; classy live music; crepe recipes (on the CD-ROM)

Major expenses: Ingredients for crepes

Primary source of income: Reservations (about $15 per person)

Benefits: Different and challenging project, potential for large profit

This fundraiser requires a lot of hard work and preparation; but if done well, the event brings in a lot of money. Costs are low, and you can charge big bucks because the experience is so unique and classy. And the formal atmosphere provides a different kind of fellowship from that which people usually experience at church.

Plan for an elegant evening. Ask members of your church whether you can borrow fine china, crystal, and silverware. Set up card tables, and place tablecloths and candles on them. Find a string quartet, jazz combo, violinist, harpist, pianist, or classical guitarist who is willing to perform for free or for tips. (Look to your congregation and youth group first.) Students who work as servers should wear white shirts, black pants or skirts, and black ties and provide full and formal service. In your advertisements, mention that guests should come "dressed to the nines." Create an elegant mood in every way possible, down to garnishes on the plates and beautifully folded napkins.

Provide two crepe entrees. Side items might include a salad. Then serve dessert crepes. (See the CD-ROM for recipes, or use your own.)

Your group can do almost all of the work a day in advance (perhaps all night before the event). Ask all helpers whether they have a crepe pan; if so, ask them to bring it to the cooking session. (These pans help especially with dessert crepes, which should be very thin.)

At cooking time, put the youth in an assembly line, with one person dipping the batter into the pan and cooking one side. When that side is cooked, he or she can flip the crepe into the next pan and someone else can cook the other side. When crepes have cooled, stack them in between sheets of wax paper and refrigerate them.

The night of the crepe dinner, heat the fillings. A few minutes before you dish out the fillings, take the crepes out of the refrigerator, so that they will reach room temperature. The filling will warm them up.

Have the guests make reservations and order their crepes ahead of time by checking off what they want from a fancy-looking menu. (Use the menu provided on the CD-ROM, or have youth create a customized menu for your event.) Charge about $15 per person, with a reduced price for children.

CUTEST-BABY-PICTURE CONTEST

Setting: In your church building or at another location familiar to members of your congregation

Supplies: Lots of baby pictures of members of your congregation; prizes such as rattles or sippy cups

Major expenses: None

Primary source of income: Votes for the cutest baby picture

Benefits: No overhead costs; the reminder that we all came into this world as innocent little babies

Have you ever wondered what your senior pastor looked like as a baby? What about the choir director? the oldest person in your congregation? This fundraiser gives you an excuse to find out what church leaders and other members of your congregation looked like as infants.

Solicit baby pictures from the pastoral staff, youth staff, volunteers, Sunday school teachers, music ministers, and any other church members who have an adorable or memorable picture of themselves as a baby or toddler. Give each picture a number, and display the pictures on a wall, table, bulletin board, or posterboard. (Keep a secret list that says which numbers correspond with which pictures.)

The objective of this fundraiser is to determine who has the cutest baby picture, and people vote with their money. In your advertising, clearly state that people need to bring cash or checkbooks to the event. Periodically announce which photo is in the lead, so that people who feel strongly about another baby picture can get on the ball and vote some more.

And the end of the event, announce whose photos won and give out some fun baby-related prizes (such as rattles or sippy cups). Also let the voters know how much money they have contributed to your youth ministry.

DANCE

Setting: An evening in your church's fellowship hall or at another location familiar to many in your congregation and community

Supplies: Decorations, costumes, promotional materials

Major expenses: Decorations, costumes

Primary source of income: Ticket sales, refreshment sales, or both

Benefit: Potential community outreach

Host a dance for a large gathering of youth or an intergenerational group. Hire a DJ, recruit youth to take charge of music, find a live band, or plug an MP3 player into a sound system and hit the "shuffle" button. Select a special theme, such as the fifties or the twenties, play the music, and learn the dances of the era. Or, if you can find a caller, have an old-fashioned barn dance featuring square dancing. (Try to have the event in an old barn and offer hot apple cider and bobbing for apples.) Sell tickets or charge a small admission fee; you could also sell refreshments.

The group you are targeting will determine where and how your promote the event, whether by e-mail, fliers in your church, or contacting other churches and community centers in your area. Organize so that the patrons have a good experience and will come back for other dances in the future.

Create an inviting and exciting atmosphere in your dance hall by using decorations related to the theme. If your theme lends itself to costumes, make sure that all of the youth who are working the event are appropriately dressed.

If your dance is open to youth from the community, consider holding it after a home basketball or football game at a nearby high school.

Testimonial: Moonlighter's Dance

Our youth group does several fundraising projects each year, but the one the congregation likes the most is the Moonlighter's Dance.

We have the dance every February, and it's a big affair. The event is named for the Moonlighters Band, a big-band swing group that plays at the dance every year. The Moonlighters Band has made our fundraiser an annual gig, and the congregation looks forward to the band's performance each winter. Though the style of music stays the same from year to year, we always have different themes. For instance, the theme for the most recent dance was the 1930s. A few years ago, we went with a 1980s theme, so there were lots of leg warmers and sweatbands on the dance floor. We gather at the church on the morning of the dance to put up decorations that will help create the right mood. The combination of consistency (having the Moonlighters play) and novelty (a new theme each year) has made the Moonlighters Dance an ongoing success.

We sell tickets in advance, starting several weeks before the day of the dance. Tickets are available before and after worship, and several of us go around to the adult Sunday school classes to tell them about the dance and sell tickets. The money we raise goes to our youth ministry and helps fund mission trips and provide scholarships for the youth who go on these trips.

The dance draws people of all generations, and it has become a wonderful way for members of the congregation to socialize and get to know one another better. In addition to being an effective fundraiser, the Moonlighters dance has become a great way to strengthen the congregation's sense of community.

I think that the essence of the Moonlighter's Dance is not dancing, listening to great music, or even raising money but knowing that our congregation is a community that appreciates being together and supporting our young people. Overall, I think that this event is one of our best traditions and will continue to be something that people look forward to because they know that it is more than just a fundraiser.

Contributed by Hannah Plummer, a youth at Belmont United Methodist Church in Nashville, Tennessee.

SENIOR PROM

Setting: A Saturday evening in your fellowship hall or another space familiar to members of your congregation

Supplies: Theme decorations, music (either a DJ or a band), refreshments, napkins, cups, eating utensils

Major expenses: Decorations, food, rental of a space (optional)

Primary source of income: Ticket sales

Benefit: Great opportunity for church members of several generations to interact with one another

Do you have a congregation filled with fun-loving grandmas and grandpas? Then why not host a "senior" prom? Invite everyone in your congregation to an elegant evening of dinner and dancing where the older adults are the honored guests and the youngsters are the chaperones . . . and the cooks, the servers, and the clean-up crew.

Advertise and beginning selling tickets well in advance. Sell individual tickets rather than couples tickets out of consideration for widows, widowers, and other singles. Choose decorations that will set a festive and nostalgic mood. Your décor might hearken back to a period familiar to the older adults in your congregation, such as the 1940s or 1950s. Find a DJ or band that can play music from that time period and throw in a few songs that appeals to all generations. Consider providing prom pictures to the guests.

Marie Zumalt and Bill Coats dance the night away at the "senior" prom at Kimberling City United Methodist Church in Kimberling City, Missouri.

Testimonial

Kendra Fredrickson, the youth minister at Kimberling City United Methodist Church in Kimberling City, Missouri, who does the "senior" prom as an annual fundraiser, says:

> Our church family loves this intergenerational annual event, and the youth usually net between $600 and $750 for our mission trip. Our theme is "A Night to Remember," and we decorate with memorabilia from the 1940s through the 1990s. We use old prom dresses, albums—yes, albums—yearbooks, hats, gloves, radios, and, of course, tons of twinkling lights. We even have a disco ball for the dance floor! Our youth dress up in their prom dresses and suits—sometimes even in groovy thrift-shop finds. Our "seniors" really get into it too! We see couples in evening gowns and tuxedos and even corsages! Our DJ (a dad) plays a variety of music, from big band to disco to country to pop; and one of our students takes pictures of every guest or couple. As a thank you, we give away "senior" photos.
>
> While this dance is a great fundraiser for us, it has become much more. The "senior" prom puts adults and students together in a fun, non-threatening way. It's not uncommon to see moms and sons, fathers and daughters, and seventy-year-olds with seventeen-year-olds laughing and learning and dancing together.

READY-TO-GO FUNDRAISERS

DOLLARS FOR MILES

Setting: At your church, weeks or months leading up to a big trip

Supplies: A visual aid that illustrates how many miles of your trip have been paid for; cash box and change

Major expenses: None

Primary source of income: Donations

Benefits: This low-cost fundraiser lets people know exactly how far their donations are going.

Many youth fundraisers are done in hopes of paying for a trip, whether it's a mission trip, a pilgrimage to a denominational gathering, or a journey to a Christian music festival. This fundraiser is specifically for such trips. It does not involve selling anything but helps people understand exactly what their money is paying for.

Begin by creating a large visual aid. Enlist a team of computer-savvy and artistic youth to carry out this task. The creation should feature a van, bus, plane, or other form of transportation and a line leading from your church to your destination. You'll need some way to chart progress along this line, such as by making the van or plane a separate piece that you can move.

Calculate the total amount of money you will need to pay for your trip, and divide this amount by the number of miles you will travel. Divide this cost per mile by the number of people going on the trip. Then advertise what it will cost for one person to travel one mile or for the entire group to travel one mile, and sell miles. Do not give donors the option of buying miles for a specific person; instead distribute the money evenly or as need dictates. Keep track of miles as they are paid for by using your visual aid.

EASTER-BASKET SERVICE

Setting: Throughout Lent in your congregation

Supplies: Baskets, candy, healthful options for the nutritional basket, (described below), markers to decorate eggs, construction paper, hole punch, string, colored markers, decorative tags, paper Easter grass, cellophane, ribbon, order forms (on the CD-ROM), cash box and change

Major expenses: Baskets, treats, supplies

Primary source of income: Easter-basket orders

Benefit: Helping parents and other adults give a child an Easter basket

This fundraiser puts a smile on children's faces and saves busy parents (and grandparents and Sunday school teachers) a lot of hassle.

Throughout Lent, take orders for the Easter baskets. Reach the adults in your congregation by visiting Sunday school classes, sending messages through Sunday school e-mail lists, and putting notices in the church newsletter and in bulletins. Make the price per basket high enough to make a profit but not so high that the parents will consider the baskets too expensive.

For each basket, decorate the eggs with the child's name. Also, attractively write the child's name on a decorative tag, punch a hole in the tag, and attach the tag to the basket by using a string.

Give customers the choice of a traditional basket, which includes the usual Easter candy, or a nutritional basket, which includes only healthful items. Many parents try to limit their children's sugar intake and would appreciate the nutritional basket.

In the nutritional basket, put decorated hard-boiled eggs; individually wrapped granola bars; small raisin boxes; small packages of nuts; plastic eggs filled with dehydrated fruit; and apples, oranges, or other fresh fruits. Inform the customers of what will be included in the baskets, and be willing to make substitutions for items to which a child may be allergic.

Use paper Easter grass, cellophane, and ribbon to decorate the baskets. Purchase these items wholesale to make a better profit. Ask a florist or member of the congregation skilled in gift-basket arranging to teach you how to make the baskets as attractive as possible.

EASTER LILIES

Setting: In your church's sanctuary on Easter Sunday; before and after worship and Sunday school throughout Lent

Supplies: Order forms (on the CD-ROM), lilies, cash box and change

Personnel needed: A few adult volunteers to help deliver lilies

Major expenses: Flowers

Primary source of income: Lily orders

Benefit: Providing lovely Easter décor for your sanctuary

Lilies, symbols of the resurrection and new life, decorate sanctuaries Easter morning. And these flowers provide an excellent opportunity for fundraising.

Throughout Lent, take orders for Easter lilies from members of the congregation. The order forms should include the names of the givers and the name of the persons to whom or for whom the lily is being given. (You might offer the choice of "in memory of" or "in honor of.") The forms should also indicate whether the donors will pick up the plants after the Easter service or allow you to give them away.

Give the collected forms to someone in the church who can organize the information and place it in the church bulletin or post it elsewhere. Well before Easter, order the lilies. Have them delivered the Saturday before Easter. Have the youth work with the church's worship committee to arrange the plants in the sanctuary.

After the service, make sure that all of the lilies that are being picked up have been claimed. Have a team of youth and adult leaders deliver any unclaimed plants to members of the church who were unable to attend the Easter service.

ECO DINNER

Setting: Evening or weekend afternoon at your church building or a location familiar to most people in your community

Supplies: Environmentally friendly menu items, dishes, napkins, and so forth; information sheet on conserving natural resources (on the CD-ROM); cash box and change

Major expenses: Food

Primary source of income: Admission fee

Benefit: Educating church members about tending to God's creation

An eco-dinner provides a fun way to conclude a study on stewardship and our call to care for creation. Choose a simple menu, such as spaghetti, salad, bread, dessert, and beverages; do your best to use organic ingredients that have been grown in a manner that is friendly to the surrounding environment. If you can find reusable dishes, silverware, and napkins, use them instead of disposable products. (Consider using candlelight to show how nice saving electricity can be.)

Offer discounts on the admission price to guests who bring a bag of recyclable materials. For example, admission may be $10 or $5 plus a bag of recyclables. Specify on your advertising what items are acceptable. Check with your local recycling drop-off stations to see what types of plastic and cardboard they will accept and what conditions apply (such as no paper with glue or only containers that have been rinsed). Make arrangements to transport the recyclable items after the meal.

Publicize the eco-dinner several weeks in advance, so that the guests will have plenty of time to collect recyclables. When people bring their items to the dinner, gather them so that the patrons can see how much waste they have saved.

Find ways during the meal to educate people about recycling and other ways to conserve natural resources (such as how much water is saved by turning off the faucet while brushing one's teeth). The CD-ROM provides a sheet of conservation facts.

Also consider inviting a guest speaker to speak about conservation and stewardship of God's creation.

FALL FESTIVAL

Setting: An indoor or outdoor space on your church property or elsewhere in your community on Halloween or a Saturday before or after Halloween

Supplies: Food, games, activities, cash box and change

Major expenses: Food

Primary sources of income: Admission fee, food sales

Benefit: Providing a fun and safe way to celebrate Halloween

People celebrate Halloween in various ways; some don't recognize the holiday at all. With the loss of neighborhoods where residents know everyone else and feel safe, trick-or-treating is on the decline in some places. Still, the beautiful month of October is a great time for a celebration.

Sponsor a fall festival for your congregation or community, including games, goodies, and costumes. Serve a simple meal such as hamburgers or hot dogs, or provide traditional fair food such as funnel cakes or corn fritters. (Provide some healthful options as well.) Have a costume contest that encourages participants to avoid traditional demons and witches and come up with disguises that require more creativity. You might even have a "heroes of the faith" category for the costume contest.

Begin planning for the festival in early September. Reserve a large space in your church building or elsewhere in the community, or find an appropriate outdoor setting. Advertise several weeks in advance, and mention what food will be sold or served and the admission price (if you choose to have one) in all promotional materials.

RENT A BOOTH AT A FALL FESTIVAL

Setting: A fall festival in or near your community

Supplies: A rented space, something to sell or an activity to oversee, any related supplies, a tent or trailer (if necessary), cash box and change

Major expenses: Rental space, a tent or trailer (if necessary), supplies

Primary source of income: Sales of item (such as food), activity (such as a dunk tank), or experience (such as face painting)

Benefits: Potential for large profit; promotion of your youth ministry

Hosting your own fall festival can be fun and rewarding and can bring in a lot of money for your ministry. But putting the event together requires a lot of hard work, the commitment of a lot of people, and, in most cases, a lot of cash. If you don't have the time or resources to host a festival (or if your community has so many fall celebrations that one more would be overkill), why not participate in a festival that is already going on?

No matter where you live, there's a good chance that a nearby city or community hosts a festival of food and fun each autumn. Many of these festivals invite vendors to set up shop and sell fair foods such as fried pickles, elephant ears, candy apples, or corn fritters. Some celebrations might be tied to the harvest of specific crops, such as corn, strawberries, apples, pumpkins, or grapes. Running a booth at one of these harvest festivals can be challenging, because your way of serving a fruit or vegetable must stand out among the other offerings. And you'll need to learn what permit (if any) is required for selling food at such an event in your state or locale.

But fall festivals are about much more than food. Some well-known adults in the community could sit in a "dunk tank," and your teens could charge people a set amount for three chances to hit the target. Your group could also run a face-painting booth or set up an area where children can carve and decorate pumpkins that their families buy for a reasonable price.

Running a booth at a fall festival often involves renting a space. Since these events are almost always outdoors, you may also need to rent a tent or

trailer to serve as your booth. If you participate in the same festival year after year, investing in your own tent or trailer may be wise.

FAMILY FUN NIGHT

Setting: An evening in your church's fellowship hall or at another location familiar to your congregation and community

Supplies: Several board games and table games, snacks, change and cash box

Major expenses: Snacks

Primary source of income: Admission fee

Benefit: Fun for the congregation

With your students and a team of adults, plan and supervise a tournament of board games. Designate one room for various popular board games, and another space for those who are not competing in the tournament. Offer table tennis, table soccer, and other such games as space permits. Have the youth work as supervisors.

Charge $2.00 or $3.00 per person. Allow people to form teams for the tournament of board games when they arrive, but also give them the opportunity to get a team together beforehand and sign their team up for the tournament. Recruit adult Sunday school classes to form teams in advance of the event. Offer a discount rate for teams that sign up early. (Say, $15.00 for a team of eight people.) If enough youth can supervise, you might also have a children's tournament. (Decrease or waive the admission fee for children.)

Appoint one or two people to collect admission fees at the door. Your group might sell soft drinks, cookies, popcorn, and nachos. (Have the youth work as servers and deliver snacks to players in the tournament.)

Offer prizes to the winners, such as ribbons, donated merchandise or gift certificates, or white elephants. Beforehand, ask members of the congregation or adult Sunday school classes whether they have any prizes they would like to donate.

FAT TUESDAY PANCAKE SUPPER

Setting: The Tuesday before Lent begins, in your church's fellowship hall or another location familiar to your congregation

Supplies: Pancake recipes (on the CD-ROM), tickets, pancake ingredients, mixing bowls, spoons, spatulas, condiments (butter, margarine, maple syrup, fruit syrup), fruit toppings such as strawberry and banana slices, decorations, tickets, promotional materials, coffee makers, ground coffee (caffeinated and decaffeinated), coffee filters, coffee pots, cream, sugar, tea bags, milk, juice, plates, napkins, dining utensils, cups for hot and cold beverages, cash box and change

Optional: electric griddles and extension cords, breakfast meats and skillets, chocolate sauce, whipped cream

Major expenses: Food

Primary source of income: Ticket sales

Benefit: One last feast before Lent that could begin a fun annual tradition

Make money and promote fellowship in your church and community by hosting a Fat Tuesday (also known as Shrove Tuesday or Mardi Gras) pancake supper. The patrons will have one last opportunity to stuff themselves before the beginning of Lent. And if the meal goes over well, you might decide to host an annual pancake supper that everyone can look forward to.

Begin advertising well in advance, and sell tickets before and after worship and Sunday school. Make announcements during worship, and have the youth sell tickets to adult Sunday school classes.

As Fat Tuesday approaches, have a practice session so that your youth can hone their techniques in cooking. How much batter to pour on the griddle and when to flip each pancake are best learned through trial and error.

If your church kitchen does not have a large griddle (or if your church does not have a kitchen), borrow several electric griddles from the families of your youth or other church members. If you plan on serving breakfast meats such as sausage or bacon, have plenty of skillets. Within thirty minutes before the event begins, brew coffee and, for the tea drinkers, hot water.

FESTIVAL OF GIFTS AND TALENTS

(A Fancy Way of Saying, "Talent Show")

Setting: An evening in your church's fellowship hall or another location familiar to your congregation and community

Supplies: Decorations, refreshments, vote bins, cash box and change, an emcee, teams of youth and adults to serve as stage managers, money collectors, and money counters

Major expenses: Decorations, refreshments; optional: rental sound equipment

Primary source of income: Money for votes

Benefits: Opportunity for members of the congregation to show off their talents; greater awareness of church members' gifts

Many people love the chance to perform, whether they can sing, play a musical instrument, give a humorous dramatic reading, dance, juggle, lip sync, or act out skits. Give your church that opportunity with a festival of gifts and talents. The event will encourage fellowship and generate funds for your ministry.

Start advertising and lining up acts six to eight weeks before the event. The publicity should encourage people to bring their checkbooks or several small bills, because people will vote with money for the winners. Clearly say what cause the event is supporting.

To generate interest and to line up plenty of acts, invite Sunday school classes to do group performances. Also book some members of your church staff.

Set time limits for the number of acts and the length of each act to keep the festival within a predetermined time frame. (Remember to account for time between acts.) Set a sign-up deadline for acts, and, if you can, arrange for each performer to do a sound check prior to the event.

Ready to GO

Enlist youth to serve in the following roles:

➜ **Emcee:** Invite a youth who is comfortable in front of an audience to serve as a master of ceremonies. Encourage the emcee to prepare a script that includes an introduction to each act, as well as jokes to fill the dead time that will inevitably arise.

➜ **Stage managers:** Enlist youth and adults who will make sure that the acts are ready to go on and that everything is on stage at the right time. The stage managers will need to prepare a list of what to do at certain times.

➜ **Money collectors:** Several youth will need to collect the money given for votes. These youth will also serve as moneychangers (though not of the biblical variety in Matthew 21:12-13), ready to break that ten-dollar bill into a five and five ones or to exchange four quarters for a dollar.

➜ **Money counters:** So that a winner can be determined quickly, a team of youth and adults will need to count money as soon as the time for voting has ended. If you allow the patrons to vote with their money throughout the evening (as opposed to after all of the acts have finished), money counters can periodically remove money from the voting bins and keep running totals.

FLAMINGO ATTACKS

Setting: The lawns of unsuspecting church members

Supplies: Plastic pink flamingos; cash box and change; order forms (on the CD-ROM) if needed

Major expense: Cost of flamingos

Primary source of income: Flamingo-removal fees or flamingo-attack orders

Benefits: Easy setup, a good laugh for the victims' neighbors

Plastic pink flamingos are probably the best-known and tackiest lawn ornament in the history of American landscaping. They're also a great way to raise money for your youth ministry.

The fundraiser involves playing pranks on unsuspecting households in your congregation. Here are two ways to do so:

THE SOLITARY FLAMINGO

Purchase ten to twenty pink lawn flamingos, and choose an equal number of good-humored members of your church who are home owners. Place a flamingo on each person's lawn. Tie a card to the flamingo that gives information about your ministry and why you're raising money and a number that homeowners can call to have the flamingo removed. Charge one price for flamingo removal (no more than $15) and a slightly higher price for flamingo relocation. If a victim pays for relocation, allow him or her to choose the flamingo's next destination; then repeat the process.

THE FLOCK

Announce to your congregation that for a fee (such as $20 or $30), any member of the church can have the youth group send a flock of flamingos to invade the lawn of any other church member. When someone orders "the flock," place ten or more (the more the better) plastic flamingos on the lawn of the chosen victim. After the flamingos have had at least twenty-four hours to enjoy their surroundings, remove them free of charge. You can offer this attack service anytime during the year.

Bob MacKendree, a member of Rehoboth United Methodist Church in Nashville, Tennessee, and the father of a youth, was once attacked by a flock of flamingos. He recalls, "[The flamingo attack] had a huge impact on my psyche, because that was the day my car got creamed on the freeway. The flamingoes put a more pleasing exclamation point on the day." MacKendree, who admits to ordering flamingo attacks on other homes, estimates that 100 small flamingos and eight-to-ten big ones stood in his front yard that day. "Let's just say there was a lot of pink," he says.

Bob MacKendree sits in his yard of flamingoes.

FOOD VOUCHERS

Setting: Anywhere and anytime

Supplies: Food vouchers from local restaurants, grocery stores, or both; cash box and change

Major expense: Cost of vouchers

Primary source of income: Sales of vouchers

Benefit: Vouchers are popular and practical, so this fundraiser is easy to continue once started

You can't go wrong with the popular and usable food vouchers. People have to eat; and if they buy vouchers, they will be spending no more money than they would anyway.

Here's how you make a profit: Certain stores and restaurants sell gift certificates in bulk for less than what they are worth, allowing you to keep the difference. The stores benefit from the guaranteed business. Sometimes restaurants add the enticement of a discount on certain food items. Contact grocery stores or pizza, burger, and other fast-food chains to find out whether they provide food vouchers that can be used for fundraisers.

Consider selling these gift certificates outside your congregation to the broader community.

FRIENDSHIP LINKS

Setting: At a large event such as a church bazaar or community street fair

Supplies: Construction paper, adhesive tape, table or booth at an event, cash box and change

Major expenses: Booth rental (optional)

Primary source of income: Sale of strips of paper

Benefits: Low cost, potential for building community

This fundraiser is a fun way to raise money at big events hosted by your church or your community. Cut up sheets of colored paper into strips that are 8½ inches long and 1 inch wide. (Most office supply stores sell packs of 8½" x 11" colored paper.) At the event (whether it is a street festival, church bazaar, or something else), sell the strips for a small price (no more than a dollar).

Selling strips of paper may seem odd, but the purpose of this fundraiser is not to give people paper bracelets to take home. Rather, the goal is to create the longest paper chain possible. You can challenge everyone at the event to create the world's largest paper chain. (You'll have your work cut out for you, since the current record is 54.33 miles.) Or you can assign a distinct color to each of several groups and have them compete to create the longest chain. (If you are at a church function, for example, you might assign a color to each adult Sunday school class.) Enlist a charismatic youth to make periodic announcements about the length of the paper chains and entice people to give more.

GREAT CAKE TASTING PARTY

Setting: Sunday evening

Supplies: Several great cakes (prepared by church members and friends), several copies of cake recipes, plates, utensils, coffee maker, coffee filters (caffeinated and decaffeinated), ground coffee, ice, cups for hot and cold beverages, promotional materials, cash box and change

Major expenses: Copies of the recipes, plates, utensils, cups, ground coffee

Primary source of income: Charge for admission (whether a set cost or a donation)

Benefit: The patrons get to spend an evening eating cake!

This fundraiser works especially well after a Sunday evening service.

In advance, solicit some great cakes and their recipes from church members and friends. Collect the recipes a few days ahead of time, and make several copies of each one. When the cakes are delivered, place them on long tables; place copies of a recipe beside the corresponding cake. Station one or two people behind each cake to cut it into small pieces and serve.

For the price of admission (whether a donation or a set price such as $5.00), allow each patron to taste as many cakes as he or she wants to try. The customer may also ask for and receive recipes. (You might limit the number of recipes each patron may have, considering the cost of copies. Also, consider posting each recipe on the church or youth ministry website.) Have hot coffee, milk, and ice water available.

A youth choir, an instrumental group, or soloists can provide entertainment. Find other ways to make the evening fun.

One great recipe for chocolate cream torte is available on the CD-ROM.

GREETING-CARD COMPANY

Setting: In your congregation, during a specific season or for an extended period of time

Supplies: Supplies to create handmade greeting cards, such as construction paper, card stock, decorative paper, scissors, glue sticks, hole punches, stamps, ink pads, cash box and change, plain paper, pen

Major expenses: Supplies for card making

Primary source of income: Greeting-card orders

Benefits: Giving greeting cards a personal touch in an age of fast-paced, automated communication

Despite all of the new ways of communication—mobile phones, e-mail, text messaging, instant messaging, and so on—greeting cards haven't gone out of style. And in this era of sending pictures, videos, and computer animation clips with the touch of a button, handmade cards are a special way to express sentiment.

Your group can create high-quality cards in many ways. The Internet provides a lot of ideas, as do people in your congregation who keep scrapbooks as a hobby. Stock up on construction paper, card stock, decorative papers (such as Chinese rice paper), scissors (including some special scissors that create jagged or rounded borders), hole punches that create a variety of shapes, glue sticks, rubber stamps, and other art supplies. And even though the intent is to create crafty, handmade cards, consider using computers to print out text and some graphics.

Divide the work among all of your youth. If some of them aren't into cutting and pasting, they could write greetings, take orders, or promote the sale.

Determine whether you want to do a card sale for a certain occasion (such as Christmas, Mother's Day, and Father's Day) or as an ongoing promotion for an extended period of time. Consider allowing the customers to write their own messages; or offer several messages for specific situations and relationships (such as spouses, parents, children, friends, thanks, and compassion). Determine a price that will cover your costs but will allow you to compete with other greeting card companies. Take advance orders, and have the cards crafted and delivered to the recipient within a week's time.

HALLOWEEN-PRANK INSURANCE

Setting: Several weeks leading up to Halloween (for selling policies); on November 1 at the homes of the policy holders who have claims

Supplies: Supplies that several youth and adult volunteers can use to clean up after Halloween pranksters

Personnel needed: A few adults to drive the youth to the homes of policy holders and help the group clean up

Major costs: None

Primary source of income: Sales of insurance policies

Benefits: Inexpensive setup, a service to members of the congregation

Sell Halloween prank insurance policies that will be effective on Halloween night. Prank insurance does not guarantee that no pranks will be played (although your youth ministry shouldn't be in the business of playing pranks, anyway). It does guarantee that your youth will clean soapy windows, pick up toilet paper that is within reach, dispose of smashed pumpkins, scrape eggs off the sides of houses, and take care of other perils of Halloween night festivities. Be clear about what sorts of pranks your youth will clean up after, and let the policy holders know that your prank insurance does not cover serious acts of vandalism such as broken windows or sand in gas tanks.

The policies should be paid for in advance, and the claims must be filed on November 1. The youth need to respond as quickly as possible (while working around school, homework, and extracurricular activities). The more youth who can spend an hour or so cleaning up toilet paper or smashed pumpkins, the better. You will also need several adult volunteers who are able to drive teens to the homes of policyholders. Follow your church's policy for drivers and chaperones.

HEAVENLY SUNDAE PARTY

Setting: Evening or weekend afternoon at your church building or a familiar location where a freezer is available

Supplies: Sundae ingredients and toppings (below and on the CD-ROM), nut grinder, bowls, spoons, napkins, water, other beverages, ground coffee (caffeinated and decaffeinated), coffee filters, coffee maker, cups for hot and cold beverages, ice-cream scoopers, paper table cloth, cash box and change

Major expenses: Sundae ingredients and toppings, ground coffee, bowls, spoons, and napkins

Primary source of income: Sundae sales

Benefit: Easy setup and operation

Mouths will start to water as soon as the publicity begins for this fundraiser! Purchase giant, institutional-size containers of ice cream in the basic three flavors: vanilla, chocolate, and strawberry. (Get a different flavor if you want to be adventuresome; or add a smaller container of low-fat frozen yogurt or light ice cream for patrons who are watching their fat and calorie intake.)

See the Heavenly Sundae Shopping List on the CD-ROM. The items include hot-fudge sauce (which you will need to heat somehow), caramel sauce, strawberry preserves, pineapple preserves, chocolate-shell sauce, whipped cream, nuts, cherries, banana slices, granola, and candy bits.

If you have several youth, decide ahead of time whether everyone should stick to the same job throughout the event or rotate so that everyone can have a turn at the "fun" jobs. Either way, before the party, know who is responsible for getting the supplies and for setting up. The setup includes slicing bananas any chopping up any ingredients that need grinding.

During the event, the teens will need to gather tickets at the door, serve ice cream, replenish supplies (such as toppings, water, bowls, spoons), collect dirty bowls, and wipe up spills.

To ensure efficient service, have one person at each container to scoop out ice cream as people come through the line. Place the most popular flavors first, and post a prominent menu, so that people can decide while they wait. After the customers get their ice cream, let them head to the toppings bar to build their sundae creations. Provide plenty of water, coffee, and other beverages. All of that sugar will make people thirsty.

Option: In lieu of serving sundaes, serve banana splits.

HOEDOWN

Setting: An evening in your church's fellowship hall or at another location familiar to many in your congregation and community

Supplies: Country music, decorations, food, plates, napkins, cups, beverages, and activity supplies for children

Major expenses: Food, decorations

Primary source of income: Admission fee, food sales, or donations

Benefit: Fun for the entire congregation that brings out a different side in people

Host an opportunity for the members of your church, other youth groups, and friends to come and have a country good time!

One of the most important parts of the evening is the music. Hire a live band or enlist a DJ to play down-home standards such as "Cotton-Eye Joe." If there is a square-dance club in your area, invite this group to come and help create the fun.

Plan a menu of barbeque and cold drinks. You might ask your church's men's or women's group of to host this part of the event. Or you might find a wholesale store that sells ready-made bulk quantities of barbeque and slaw.

Provide activities and organized games for young children, such as a cow-coloring or a hog-calling contest.

Tie this hoedown to the kick-off of your church's autumn programs, or make it an end-of-the-summer event. You can charge money for the food, a cover charge to enter the event, or take up a love offering at some point during the festivities. Invite the people attending to wear their western garb to add to the mood.

IN-MEMORY-OF OR IN-HONOR-OF POETRY BOOKLETS

Setting: In your congregation around Mother's Day, Father's Day, or Grandparent's Day

Supplies: Poems written by members of your congregation and classic poems (in the public domain) that can be dedicated to parents and grandparents

Major expenses: Cost of printing the books

Primary sources of income: Poem- or page-dedication fees, book sales

Benefits: A nice keepsake for church members, a way to show love and appreciation to parents and grandparents

Publish a poetry book for Mother's Day, Father's Day, Grandparent's Day, or another occasion that recognizes persons who have made an impact in our lives. A few months before the occasion, invite members of the congregation to write poems (or find poems they have already written) about their mother, father, or grandparent or a person who has been like a parent or grandparent to them. Allow these persons to buy a page of your book in honor or in memory of the person who is the subject of the poem. You might also gather classic poems about parents and grandparents that are in the public domain and allow church members to pay to dedicate a poem in honor or memory of someone. To make your books more visually appealing, have people dedicate illustrations they've done or photographs they've taken.

Have computer-savvy youth compile the poems and illustrations, along with the poets' names and dedication information, into a document that can be printed and bound. Find out how many books you need to print, and have them printed and bound by an office-supply store or copy shop or send your project to a printer. Before you advertise this fundraiser, you'll need a cost estimate, so that you can determine how much to charge for poem or page dedication, as well as the final product. This fundraiser has the potential to generate a lot of money for your ministry, but count your costs carefully to make sure that your investment doesn't outweigh the return.

INTERNATIONAL NIGHT

Setting: Evening or weekend afternoon at your church building or a location familiar to most people in your community

Personnel needed: Guest speakers of various nationalities

Supplies: Food, games, music, and decorations indigenous to the speakers' countries; beverages; plates; cups; utensils; cash box and change

Major expenses: Food, decorations

Primary source of income: Admission fee

Benefit: Education

Invite people who grew up in other countries (or lived there for several years) to talk about their lives in these lands. Feature dishes made from the speakers' countries, and display pictures of prominent landmarks in these nations and of the speakers' lives in the countries where they have lived.

Plan with the speakers ahead of time to make the experience as much fun and as educational as possible. For instance, you could ask the speakers to play a guessing game about interesting customs to warm up the audience. Questions could include, "How old do you think people in my country have to be to get a driver's license?" and "What do you think is the most popular sport in my country?" Ask the speakers whether they have any music from their countries that you could play to set the mood. Before or after the meal, play games indigenous to the countries represented. Do your best to get everyone present involved.

LIP SYNC CONTEST

Setting: An evening in your church's fellowship hall or at another location familiar to many in your congregation and community

Personnel needed: Performers

Supplies: Stage area, a sound system, décor, food (optional), cash box and change

Major expenses: Décor

Primary source of income: Ticket sales

Benefits: Fun for the entire congregation; a chance to see a side of people that you don't always see

The popularity of *American Idol* and karaoke nights have gotten Americans so interested in real singing that lip synching has become a lost art. Make a contest out of this forgotten pastime to raise money for your youth ministry.

If you are not familiar with lip synching contests, the concept is simple: Contestants mouth the words of their favorite songs while recorded music is playing.

Set up a stage, create a backdrop, and arrange for sound equipment. Advertise the event several weeks in advance. Recruit some well-known adults in the congregation such as choir members, lay leaders, and church staff to be stars of the show; but make sure that everyone feels invited, not coerced, to sign up for the contest. Ask some members of your youth group to participate as well. Remember that adults may prefer music from eras unfamiliar to the youth. While having respected elders in the congregation perform cheesy hits from the seventies and eighties is a big part of the fun, consider having some of these adults perform favorite songs of the youth in the congregation (and vice versa).

Encourage the performers to dress like the stars they are imitating. You might even make costumes part of the judges' criteria. Other categories might include precision and stage presence.

Require that all contestants submit CDs or MP3s of their music ahead of time, so that you can screen the songs for objectionable content.

MAKE MULCH OR COMPOST

Setting: A place with the necessary equipment to make mulch

Supplies: Equipment and organic clippings to make mulch; change and cash box

Major expenses: Rental of equipment to make mulch (optional)

Primary source of income: Sales of mulch

Benefit: An eco-friendly resource for local gardeners

If you want to do something good for the environment and if you have several gardeners in your congregation and community, this project is for you . . . if you have access to mulch- or compost-making equipment.

To create mulch, you'll need to fence in at least one area that is 5 or 6 feet long where you can put grass cuttings, leaves, wood chips, and anything else organic. When this area fills up, remove the mulch, put it in bags, and sell it. Mulch is spread out on top of gardens or around trees and is great for holding water in the soil, adding nutrients, and keeping weeds from growing.

Compost, like mulch, is a mixture of organic materials—though compost generally includes vegetable and fruit parings, manure, and other organic materials that decompose readily. Compost is best made in bins that can be turned over every couple of weeks to mix the layers of compost and hasten decomposition. You will also need to pour some water into the compost to help it rot. After the material in the bins has decayed, bag it and sell it. Compost is mixed with soil to help it retain moisture and to add nutrients.

Get the whole congregation involved in saving and bringing compost materials. Mulch and compost are great for gardens and puts no synthetic chemicals in the soil.

MOTHER'S DAY OR FATHER'S DAY BANQUET

Setting: On or around Mother's Day or Father's Day in your church building or another location familiar to people in your congregation and community

Supplies: Food (including appetizers and punch), plates, cups, utensils, decorations, placards featuring conversation starters, awards (optional), cash box and change

Major expenses: Food, decorations

Primary source of income: Admission fee

Benefit: The chance to honor the mothers and fathers in your congregation

Mother's Day and Father's Day are special days of the year set aside to honor our parents and show them how much we love them. Throw a banquet for mothers in your congregation on Mother's Day, and the fathers on Father's Day.

Take reservations for each banquet well in advance of the event, so that you can properly prepare. The cost will depend on what foods and beverages you offer. Designate teams of youth to decorate the tables and prepare and serve the food. Let people know ahead of time that at the banquet, everyone will have a chance to mention something special about his or her mother or father, whether or not the parent is present.

For each place setting, provide a sheet with a list of questions. (See the example on the CD-ROM.) This extra touch will encourage conversation about memories of parents and growing up.

At the event, take time to recognize special mothers and fathers, such as the oldest, the newest, and the one with the most children.

MOTHER'S DAY FLOWERS

Setting: Just outside your sanctuary on Mother's Day

Supplies: Pink or red carnations and white carnations

Major expenses: Carnations

Primary source of income: Donations

Benefits: The opportunities to keep an old tradition alive and to honor mothers

Carry on the decades-old custom of wearing a flower in honor or in memory of one's mother on Mother's Day. (Red or pink flowers symbolize that one's mother is living, and white flowers that one's mother is deceased.) Offer red or pink and white carnations to worshipers on their way into the sanctuary on Mother's Day. Ask for donations to the youth group in exchange for the flowers.

PENNY WARS

Setting: In your church building over the course of a month or a season

Supplies: Two large containers

Major expenses: None

Primary source of income: Pennies donated

Benefits: Low cost; demonstration that seemingly worthless things can have great value when they come together

A penny by itself seems worthless—not worth the energy needed to pick it up off the sidewalk or dig it out of the crevices of one's car. But pennies do have value; and if you gather enough of them, you can pay for your next youth outing one cent at a time.

To initiate a penny war, determine an issue that members of your congregation can debate. For example: Should Larry shave his legendary beard? Should Shirley dye her hair hot pink? Should the pastor put on a leisure suit or sequin dress and sing "I Will Survive" at the church picnic? (Of course, check with Larry, Shirley, or the pastor before making any of them the subject of such a debate. Also gauge your congregation's sense of humor to make sure that no one will be offended by such activities.)

Whatever the debate, the outcome will be decided with pennies. You will need two large containers to set out in your church's fellowship hall, narthex, or other gathering area. One container should be labeled "for" or "pro," and the other "against" or "con" (as in "for" Larry shaving his beard and "against" Larry shaving his beard).

You'll want to give the congregation several opportunities to donate pennies; so over the course of a month or season, encourage people to support their side of the debate by dropping pennies in the appropriate container. Make announcements during worship or other church functions to add to the drama. (For example, say, "Someone will have to bring in a few rolls of pennies soon if you don't want Shirley to come to church next week with pink hair.") Regularly mention the cause for which you're raising money, so that people feel even more compelled to part with their pennies.

At the end of the allotted time, count up the pennies, announce how much you have raised, and tell the congregation whether Larry will be losing his whiskers or the pastor will be taking a trip back to the seventies.

PEOPLE AUCTION

Setting: An evening in your church building or other location familiar to members of your congregation

Personnel needed: An auctioneer, donors who are willing to auction off their services

Supplies: Refreshments, plates, napkins, utensils, cups, decorations, entertainment to make the evening even more enjoyable (optional)

Major expenses: Food, decorations, or entertainment, depending on how much you invest in each category

Primary source of income: Bids for services

Benefits: The opportunity for youth and other members of the congregation to make good use of their skills; fellowship among church members

These days, auctions aren't limited to state fairs and art galleries. Thanks to popular online auction sites, this type of sale has become an effective way to sell everything from baby clothes to German lessons. While auctioning donated items from members of your church and community can yield high bids, auctioning donated services might prove even better.

Invite members of your congregation to think about what they might be able to donate. A skilled guitarist might donate a month's worth of lessons; someone who is handy around the house might donate certain repairs or a few hours of home-improvement work. Other donations might include babysitting, tutoring, preparing a meal, or an afternoon in a fishing boat.

Have each donor specify a time when the service will be performed (and, if necessary, a location) and suggest a minimum price for his or her service. These participants will need to provide a description of the services they are offering that the auctioneer can read aloud during the event. Also ask donors how many "items" they are willing to auction. That is, if someone is offering lessons, how many students (or auction winners) are they willing to take on?

Encourage your youth to participate and auction off their services. Many young families would love to have a couple of teenagers from the church watch their kids for an evening or watch their dog for a weekend when they're out of town. In the weeks leading up to the event, consider spending time during youth group meetings or Sunday school class helping the teens evaluate their gifts and interests and what they might be able to donate.

Promote your auction several weeks in advance, letting people know what sorts of service will be up for bids. If you can advertise the starting bids for these services, do so. Base the starting bids on the suggested minimum prices that the donors have provided. Also mention in your advertisements that cash and checks will be accepted. Ask a charismatic youth or adult to be your auctioneer; or consider finding an experienced, fast-talking auctioneer from your community.

For the auction night, have a cash box with bills and ask some youth to be moneychangers (who can break a twenty into a ten and two fives, for instance). That way, the winning bidders will be able to pay cash to the donors up front. Otherwise, they may write a check to those persons.

Set up a stage area where some donors can give people a taste of what they are offering. Someone who is donating piano lessons could play a favorite piece; someone who is offering pet-sitting services could demonstrate his or her ability to fill dog bowls and scoop cat litter. (Chewy, rolled-up chocolate candies are effective for this demonstration.) Find other ways to make the evening fun and entertaining, such as serving refreshments or having musicians perform at various times throughout the evening.

Safety is crucial to this fundraiser's success. You might limit the auction to church members and regular attendees to decrease the risk of persons with ulterior motives (such as theft or molestation) donating or purchasing services. Make sure that the youth who are donating do not wind up in a

situation where they are alone with an adult. Whenever children and youth are involved, at least two non-related adults should be present. (For example, if some youth offer a babysitting service, you could have them watch the children at the church; if some teens offer to do yard work, ask their parents to be nearby.) Your congregation's safety and security policies should apply to all church functions, even those that involve only a few members of the congregation and take place away from the church building.

POINSETTIA SALE

Setting: In your church building during the Advent and Christmas seasons

Supplies: Poinsettias, copies of the order form (on the CD-ROM), cash box and change

Major expense: Poinsettias

Primary source of income: Poinsettia orders

Benefit: Lovely Christmas décor for your sanctuary and for the living spaces of homebound members

The poinsettia, in Mexico, is called the flower of the Holy Night. Legend has it that one Christmas Eve, a boy was afraid to go to church because he didn't have anything to give to the Christ Child. He told God that he was poor and dare not approach the baby Jesus with empty hands. Immediately, a poinsettia sprouted at his feet and grew. The boy picked this flower and offered it to the Christ Child. The poinsettia, which adorns our homes and altars, reminds us of God's gifts.

For a fundraiser, take orders for poinsettias to be placed in the church sanctuary. Allow the customers to give the poinsettias in honor of or in memory of loved ones. ("In honor of" is for the living; "in memory of" is for the deceased.) The order forms should include the name of the giver, the name of the person to be honored or remembered, and whether the plant will be taken home or given away after Christmas. (See the order form on the CD-ROM.) Whoever completes the forms should take care to spell the names correctly. When all of the orders have been taken, have the list of the names of the poinsettia givers and those being honored or remembered be printed in the Sunday bulletin. You might do so by giving the list to the church secretary.

Make plans with a local florist or supermarket to buy a large quantity of poinsettias at a reasonable price. The day the flowers are purchased or delivered, arrange them in the sanctuary. Assign each of your students a time to water the plants, and ask several youth to be available on Christmas Day to deliver unclaimed poinsettias to sick and homebound members of the congregation.

POTATO BAR

Setting: An evening or weekend afternoon at your church building or a location familiar to most people in your community

Supplies: Potatoes; toppings (listed below); plates; utensils; cups; napkins; beverages; at least one long, sharp knife or a galvanized nail, cash box and change

Major expenses: Food

Primary source of income: Admission fee

Benefits: Fairly low cost, the chance for the guests to create their meals

For a meal that tastes good, try a potato-bar fundraiser. Buy large baking potatoes (as big as possible) and small ones for children; provide lots of toppings, drinks, and dessert; then turn people loose to build their toppings. Provide cheddar cheese, butter and sour cream (including low-fat varieties), ranch dressing, chives, salt, and pepper. You might also offer salsa, chili peppers, mushrooms, mushroom soup, diced tomatoes, raw onions, and stir-fried or steamed onions or green peppers. For the guests to make salads, offer a big bowl of lettuce chunks.

To ensure that the potatoes will be fully cooked on the inside, stick them all the way through several times with a long, sharp knife or galvanized nail. Wash this utensil before you stick it in the potatoes. Then wrap each potato in foil and allow it to bake at 350 degrees Fahrenheit for forty-five minutes to an hour, depending on how big it is. Ask an experienced cook to help you ensure that the potatoes are done. If the oven at your church or facility is too small, ask some people who live nearby whether you can use their ovens. If these persons agree, have them leave the foil on the spuds, wrap the potatoes in thick towels, and place them in a basket or box for the trip to the event.

RUMMAGE SALE

Setting: A Saturday morning and afternoon in your church building or another location familiar to your congregation and community

Supplies: Discarded items to sell, tables, price labels, marker, cardboard, cash box and change

Major expenses: None

Primary source of income: Sales of donated articles

Benefits: Low start-up cost, a chance for people to re-use items that would otherwise be forgotten or thrown away

The first step for planning a rummage sale is to ask members of your congregation and community to rummage through their homes, looking for any items that they no longer use or stuff they could stand to part with. You will probably have enough donations, because people are always looking to get rid of stuff that is just taking up space. So you may well end up with an assortment of miscellaneous articles that you can sell to anyone willing to spend a Saturday at your church searching for the lamp, set of patio dishes, or polyester suit that meets their needs. Ask the donors to turn in their items at least a week before the sale.

Beforehand, have a group of youth work together to come up with a price system. Determine a base price for each type of item (such as electronics, shirts, coats, furniture, cookware, and baby clothes). The youth can then raise or lower the price according to the condition of individual items. Have the youth gather on an evening prior to the sale to sort and price the items and set them out on tables. For delicate items, the teens may make small cardboard signs to display the prices instead of placing stickers on the merchandise.

Hold the sale on a Saturday, and stay open for much of the morning and afternoon. Promote the sale throughout your community. Put fliers on grocery store bulletin boards, post messages on Internet forums, take out an ad in the local paper, and ask your congregation to spread the word. If any big-ticket items (such as large appliances or pieces of furniture) have been donated, mention them in your advertising.

SATURDAY FUN DAY

Setting: A Saturday afternoon in your church building or another space in your neighborhood

Supplies: Snacks, beverages, napkins, plates, cups, art-and-craft supplies, other materials for children's activities, cash box and change, plastic gloves

Personnel needed: At least one adult to be on site; adults who work with your church's children's ministry (optional)

Major expenses: Cost of snacks and any materials for arts, crafts, and activities that your church doesn't already have

Primary source of income: Reservation fee

Benefits: This fundraiser allows the youth to connect with the children, who look up to them; if you do these fun days often, they can attract young families looking for a church home.

Offer children a treat (and give parents a break) by sponsoring regular Saturday afternoon fun days for the children in your congregation and their friends. If your church is located in a residential area, open these days to kids in the community. Ask the parents to make advance reservations for their children, so that you know how many to expect. Tell the parents that the fee covers babysitting and food. Require all parents who drop off their children to leave emergency contact information, preferably including a mobile-phone number.

Plan creative games and art projects; include activities that involve physical exercise. Provide healthful refreshments. (If you avoid treats and beverages that contain large quantities of sugar, the energy level will be more manageable.) You might even enlist the help of the older children in preparing some of these snacks. Make sure that everyone who is preparing food wears plastic gloves (or at the very least washes his or her hands thoroughly).

If you decide to offer these fun days on a regular basis, do some research on positive discipline. Consider asking adults who work with your congregation's children's ministry to help out with your fun days.

SINGING TELEGRAMS

Setting: Over the phone, on the Web, and anywhere your youth can quickly and safely travel to

Supplies: Order forms, gift baskets and flowers (optional), cash box and change (optional)

Personnel needed: An adult to travel with every four singers

Major expenses: Gift baskets and flowers if you choose to offer them, and gasoline if you deliver the telegrams to homes

Primary source of income: Telegram sales

Benefits: Showcase of your group's musical ability, minimal investment

If your youth like to sing, consider starting an ongoing singing-telegram service. You could offer telegrams over the phone, deliver telegrams in person, or (if your youth are tech savvy) send out a weblink or put out a podcast of the telegram. Decide which of these options you will offer and when the telegrams may be delivered.

If you want these messages delivered in person, divide the youth into groups of four who can sing the telegrams. Make sure that these youth travel with at least one adult. Also put some youth in charge of taking orders and getting the home address (with directions), e-mail address, phone number, or whatever information is needed for delivery.

If you opt for digital-age singing telegrams that will be delivered online, find a youth or adult who can record them and someone who can set up the podcast or other electronic delivery system. Use an Internet payment service such as PayPal to collect money.

As you continue offering this service, teams of youth will develop their own vocal style and presentation, and church members will request certain youth for certain types of telegrams.

Have the youth create arrangements of old standards (such as "Happy Birthday" and "You Are My Sunshine") and appropriate pop songs. Creative members of your group might compose songs for specific situations. Offer telegrams for as many situations as possible, including the following:

➜ Birthdays   ➜ "I love you"
➜ Holidays   ➜ "I'm sorry"
➜ Friendship   ➜ "Have a good day"

If you want this service to be an ongoing fundraiser, the youth will need to commit to continuous practice. The longer you offer this service, the better you'll get and the more telegrams you'll be able to offer.

SINGING CHRISTMAS-GRAMS

Setting: Around town on an evening during Advent; before and after worship and Sunday school on Sundays leading up to the event

Supplies: Singers, order forms, transportation, permission forms

Major expenses: Gasoline

Primary source of income: Christmas-gram orders

Benefits: A new dimension to the tradition of caroling; connection with members of the congregation; a lot of fun

Do your youth like to go caroling and spreading Christmas cheer each December? If they don't, do you make them do it anyway? If caroling is a yearly tradition for you and your teens, try making it a fundraiser.

Several weeks before you go caroling, tell members of your congregation that they can send a special Christmas greeting to someone by hiring your carolers to sing that person a song. When you take orders, get the name and address of the recipient and, if need be, directions to that person's house. You might also ask for the person's phone number so that you can be sure that he or she will be home to receive your singing Christmas-gram. (When you call, try not to let the person know that you are about to visit and sing Christmas carols.)

Once all of the orders are in, map out your route. If you have a lot or orders and the homes are spread out, you may need to carol on multiple nights. When you arrive at one of the designated homes, greet the Christmas-gram recipient by name and tell him or her who has sent the greeting. Try to make plenty of unpaid stops along the way, singing to homebound persons, older adults in your congregation, church members you haven't seen in a while, and other people to whom you want to give a Christmas blessing.

Involve as many youth as possible in this activity. If a youth doesn't sing but plays guitar, invite him or her to accompany the group. If a youth plays an instrument such as the trumpet or flute, he or she might perform a solo in some of the carols. Other youth might shake bells or wear appropriate costumes to set the mood.

SINGING VALENTINES

Setting: Over the phone and anywhere your youth can quickly and safely travel to

Supplies: Order forms, gift baskets and flowers (optional)

Major expenses: Gift baskets and flowers (if you choose to offer them), gasoline for delivering telegrams to houses

Primary source of income: Singing-Valentine sales

Benefits: Minimal investment, showcase of your youth group's musical ability

This fundraiser helps people show their appreciation to friends and loved ones on Valentine's Day. For several weeks prior to that day, spread the word that people can hire your group to deliver singing Valentines. If you can handle the business, you may want to advertise in the community as well. Decide when you will deliver the messages and what kind of services to offer, such as

→ singing over the phone;
→ singing in person;
→ delivering a plate (wrapped in red cellophane) of Valentine cookies or banana bread;
→ delivering a gift basket (wrapped in red cellophane) filled with cheeses or low-fat spreads and crackers, chocolates, or fruit, and including a poem;
→ delivering a rose or carnation.

Price each of these components separately. Consider distances of driving when you decide on prices.

Next, choose what songs you will offer. Pick some old standards as well as some current hits, making sure that you have something for every generation. In addition to romantic tunes, offer some songs about friendship. Teenage guitarists could serve as accompanists. Spend plenty of time practicing the songs, and work on harmonization where it is possible. You might have the performers do dances or motions for effect.

SOCCER CAMP

Setting: A week during the summer, on your church's lawn or at a local school or park

Supplies: One soccer ball and one pinny for every child who participates; clean garbage cans; soccer goals; water; snacks; first-aid supplies; basic information sheet, health form, liability waiver (on the CD-ROM); pens; a few sheets of paper

Personnel needed: At least one adult volunteer for every three youth working the camp, a few strong people, someone with truck or bed trailer, adult certified in first aid and CPR

Major expenses: Soccer balls, goals (if you need to buy them), snacks

Primary source of income: Registration fee

Benefits: Youth develop leadership skills by working with children, provide a service to children in your community

Soccer is probably the most popular sport in the world. And even though many Americans are more interested in football, basketball, and baseball, soccer has grown in popularity among children and youth in the US. The game is simple to teach, easy to learn, and fun to play. It teaches players teamwork and patience, and it's a great way to get outdoor exercise.

With your youth group, hold a week-long summer soccer camp. Look for teens who play soccer for their schools or club teams, and invite these youth to play a leadership role in setting up the camp. Arrange for times when your soccer experts can teach their peers the ins and outs of the game. Consider providing books and other reading material for volunteers who aren't familiar with soccer, or have them read about soccer on the Internet. You might also request an official rule book from your state's school athletic association.

Find a large outdoor space to hold your camp. If you are allowed to use spray paint, mark off the boundaries to a soccer field in your church's yard. If your church doesn't have enough outdoor property, contact local parks or schools about using their fields. (And make sure that you have access to restrooms.) Since soccer goals can be expensive, check with parks or schools about borrowing or renting goals for a week. For hauling the goals, you'll need a truck or bed trailer and some strong members of your congregation.

Purchase several new soccer balls, and store them in clean garbage cans. You'll also need pinnies (brightly colored jerseys with a slit down the side, held together by two straps); the kids can slip them on over their shirts when breaking up into teams. Have a ball and pinny for every participant, as well as plenty of water and some snacks. Since injuries sometimes happen in soccer, keep first-aid supplies on hand and make sure that someone certified in CPR and first aid is present at all times.

Add up your expenses, and determine a registration fee for the camp. (Consider offering scholarships or discounts for kids from low-income households.) Aim for a ratio of three children for every teen volunteer. This measure may mean cutting off registration after a certain point; but if you take too many kids, you'll be overwhelmed and things will get out of control. You should also have at least one adult volunteer for every three youth working at the camp.

As a part of your sign-up, include a basic information sheet, a health form, and a liability waiver. See the CD-ROM for examples. In this sign-up packet, include clear rules and expectations for both the participants and the parents. Check with your state and local government to see whether you need any special permits or permissions to hold this kind of camp. Your local health-and-safety department may also need to inspect your facilities.

When the players arrive each day for the camp, have their parents sign them in and send them to their coaches. Begin each day with a devotion, including a prayer and a Bible memory verse. The verses might focus on perseverance (as in **Hebrews 12:1-2**), working together (as in **1 Corinthians 12:4-6**), or honoring the body (as in **1 Corinthians 6:19-20**). Go over your rules at the beginning of each day, and be clear about what the consequences will be for broken rules.

Break your camp into blocks of time, and assign each team a name or number. Blow a whistle to indicate when teams should switch from one area to another. You might have a few different drill stations, a scrimmage game, a snack area, and a Bible-story area. Work out a schedule that keeps everyone busy and having fun.

End each day with prayer and a revisiting of your Bible memory verse. Send home to the kids' parents a sheet with the Bible verse and a summary of what the kids did that day.

Contributed by Theresa Noel, the youth minister at Forrest Hill United Methodist Church in Peoria, Illinois. Theresa's youth group runs an annual soccer camp for children that is fun, rewarding, and a great way to raise money.

SOUTHERN NIGHT

Setting: Evening or weekend afternoon at your church building or a location familiar to most people in your community

Supplies: Food, plates, dining utensils, napkins, beverages, cups, regional decorations, entertainment such as music and dance, cash box and change

Major expenses: Food, decorations

Primary source of income: Ticket sales

Benefits: A lot of fun, good food, potential to make a lot of money

For a memorable food fundraiser, try a Southern Night or a theme dinner focused on another part of the country.

Southern Night should be about good food entertainment. Serve dishes from the South (or the state or region of your choice). Ask family, friends, and church members to contribute dishes for the meal. Arrange appetizers, entrees, and desserts on different tables, and arrange the tables in a way that will ease traffic flow.

Here are some suggestions for a Southern-themed dinner: seafood (shrimp, catfish, or croaker), fried chicken, biscuits, cole slaw, vegetables such as fried okra and green beans, and desserts such as pecan pie with vanilla ice cream. See the CD-ROM for recipes.

Decorate the space festively. Place fresh flowers, candles and glass hurricane candle holders, or magnolia leaves on each table.

Enlist people to entertain the customers. Focus on variety, but stay true to the theme. Have regional music (which, for the South, could include blues, bluegrass, gospel, and country), dances, and storytelling. Display regional art such as paintings of southern landscapes, basketry, or quilts. Also create a mini market so that the people can sell their merchandise (either crafts or garage-sale items) that fit the theme. (Think of a country gift store.)

Sell tickets for the event at least a month in advance. Organize committees to be responsible for room arrangement, food, talent, and the mini market. Involve as many youth and people from the congregation as possible.

Send each guest home with a souvenir such as a can of peaches, scuppernongs (wild grapes), or shelled pecans.

STRAWBERRY PATCH

Setting: Throughout the growing season for strawberries, culminating in a strawberry festival on a weekend afternoon at your church or another location familiar to most people in your community

Supplies: Four committees of youth, strawberry plants, gardening supplies, recipes including strawberries, promotional materials, menus, cash box and change

Major expenses: Strawberry plants and gardening supplies

Primary source of income: Sales of strawberries and strawberry dishes

Benefits: Some youth will better understand where their food comes from and develop new skills.

If you live in a part of the country where strawberries grow, plan a strawberry festival. Eating fresh fruit is one of the best ways to enjoy spring and summer. Give your community an opportunity to pick their own fruit. Celebrate by preparing strawberry dishes and a collection of recipes.

This activity requires time and work, but it can be fun and profitable. First, decide whether to grow strawberries or pick them from a local farmer's crop. Then select four work committees: gardeners (or pickers), publicity, hospitality, and sales.

If your group is going to grow strawberries, locate a piece of land. Someone you know, such as a member of your congregation, may be willing to share a plot. Ask around. Once the property is selected, find an experienced gardener to supervise the work. The gardening committee, with the help of the gardener, will need to determine how many plants will fit in your garden. Members of the committee will also plant the strawberries and cultivate the soil until the harvest. These youth may need to place nets over the garden to keep birds from eating the crop.

As the strawberries ripen, the publicity committee will take the lead in advertising your strawberry festival. The committee can post a notice on the church website, advertise in local newspapers, send messages to local bloggers whose readers may have some interest in the event, post fliers in area businesses, and prepare personal cards of invitation for family and friends. Have computer-savvy youth and artistically inclined youth work together on any ads or fliers. Personalize any individual invitations. Include in all advertisements who, what, when, where, and how much.

The hospitality committee will select some strawberry dishes to prepare for the festival. Some simple recipes might include strawberry preserves, fresh strawberries with whipped cream, or strawberry shortcake. Have the youth design a special menu in the shape of a strawberry that lists the items for sale at the festival and their prices; and have computer savvy and artistically inclined youth work together to create a book of strawberry recipes that you can sell at the festival.

In the days and weeks leading up to the festival, the hospitality committee will design the serving area. You might use outdoor tables and chairs, or scatter picnic tables across the area. The hospitality committee might also design souvenirs such as T-shirts or buttons.

Finally, the sales committee will set prices for all the items sold at the festival. The committee should price the strawberries according to weight or volume (per pound or per pint, for example) and should do research on the Internet to come up with reasonable prices for the other items.

This festival idea can also work well with pecans, peaches, and blueberries. Choose fruits that aren't plentiful but can be grown in your area. If it is a success, make the festival an annual event.

SUPER-BOWL SUBS

Setting: Early morning on Super Bowl Sunday (preparation) and after worship on Super Bowl Sunday (pick up and delivery)

Supplies: Ingredients; order form and shopping list (on the CD-ROM); plastic gloves for each sandwich artist; plastic wrap; adhesive label for each sub; markers; cash box and change; cooler and ice (optional)

Major expenses: Ingredients for the sandwiches

Primary source of income: Sandwich sales

Benefits: Ready-made customer base, fun preparation, tie to a major event

Making and selling Super Bowl submarine sandwiches to the congregation can become a yearly tradition. Fans will appreciate having this tasty (and already prepared) meal as they watch the big game on television. Several weeks in advance, take orders at church, by e-mail, or by phone; or post the form on the church or youth group website. Use the order form provided on the CD-ROM, or create one of your own. Give a discount for prepaid orders.

On the order sheets, let the customers choose their ingredients and size of sandwich. Offer a variety of sandwich meats, cheeses, dressings, and fresh vegetables. See the shopping list and order form on the CD-ROM for suggested ingredients.

To ensure competitive prices, make them comparable to those at local delis or grocery stores. Encourage buying by offering discounts for orders of five or more subs. Check with food wholesalers or warehouse stores about purchasing ingredients, condiments, and plastic wrap or foil at quantity discount prices. Merchants in your congregation may be willing to donate some of these items.

Gather early in the morning on Super Bowl Sunday to prepare the subs. (Finish before worship starts.) Prepare according to the selections made on the order forms. To ensure repeat business, make high-quality sandwiches. Include in each sub, for instance, 1½ ounces each of two meats and a cheese, onion slices, banana peppers, and two tomato slices. Label each wrapped sub with the customer's name, and keep the subs in alphabetical order.

Make plenty of extra sandwiches for impulse buyers. Keep them in a refrigerator or in coolers. Churchgoers can pick up the sandwiches after worship. You will need to deliver orders received from people outside the church.

Have your own sub-and-Super-Bowl party after the deliveries are done.

TASTE-AND-TELL LUNCHEON

Setting: Saturday or Sunday afternoon in your church building or a location familiar to most people in your community

Supplies: Several teaspoons, dishes and silverware, napkins, beverages, favorite dishes prepared by various members of the congregation, paper, hole punch, staples or string for binding the booklets, cash box and change, thank-you or blank cards, pen, stamps

Major expenses: None

Primary source of income: Ticket sales

Benefits: Low overhead, easy preparation

Taste-and-tell luncheons introduce people to delicious new dishes while bringing in lots of money. Plan this event for a time when people can easily attend, such as a weekend afternoon. Decide how many meat dishes, vegetables, salads, breads, and desserts you want to have. Then ask youth and adult Sunday school classes and men's and women's groups to submit copies of their favorite recipes and to prepare two dishes of their chosen recipe for the taste-and-tell luncheon. After the event, send thank-you notes to everyone who has contributed.

Get copies of everyone's recipes far enough in advance that the recipes can be combined into a small booklet for everyone who attends. On long tables, spread out one of each dish, and use teaspoons as serving spoons. (Remember that this event is a tasting party.) Ideally, there will be so many entries that people's plates will be piled high with teaspoonfuls of these culinary delights. Keep the second dish of each recipe in the kitchen to bring out when the first one is gone.

Set a limit on the number of customers. Sell tickets in advance, so that you will know how much food to have and how many recipe booklets to prepare. Plan to have a few extra for people who show up at the door.

T-SHIRT SALE

Setting: In your congregation

Supplies: An attractive T-shirt design that promotes your church, custom-made T-shirts featuring this design, cash box and change

Major expense: The cost of getting T-shirts made

Primary source of income: T-shirt sales

Benefits: Promoting your congregation, providing church groups with matching shirts for outings

We live in a T-shirt-wearing society. Many Americans have drawers full of these collarless short-sleeved garments and especially like tees that represent something they consider important. For instance, people like to wear shirts that promote their favorite band, sports team, or brand of clothing. Travelers often pick up a souvenir T-shirt before returning home. School clubs and athletic teams commonly get shirts made for their members. Shirts featuring sayings or characters from popular television shows or movies are especially popular among youth. (Remember the *Napoleon Dynamite*-inspired "Vote for Pedro" fad from a few ago?) In recent years, T-shirts designed especially for Christian teens have become commonplace.

All this is to say: People want T-shirts, especially ones that express their likes, interests, and values. So why not make T-shirts that promote your congregation? Have the youth submit designs and hold a contest where members of the congregation choose their favorite. Better yet, invite all of the youth who are interested in designing the T-shirt to work together on a design each of them is happy with.

Estimate how much the T-shirts will cost, and set your price. The cost will depend on how many you order, so determine a reasonable goal for shirt sales. Display your T-shirt design on a posterboard or foam board, and take advance orders. Talk with various groups in your church (such as the choir and the men's or women's groups) about purchasing a shirt for each member so that they can identify themselves when they go on outings. Try to get some additional shirts made for people who didn't place orders. You might sell these extras at a slightly higher price once the shirts come in.

For more information on ordering custom-made T-shirts and other items, see "Cokesbury Specialty Imprints" on pages 102–103.

TREASURE HUNT

Setting: An evening or afternoon beginning in your church building and emanating into the neighborhood or community

Supplies: Prepared clues, prizes, cash box and change

Personnel needed: Adult volunteer

Major expenses: Prizes (if they are not donated)

Primary source of income: Entry fee

Benefit: A fun and challenging competition

As you can see in popular movies and TV shows, Americans love to investigate, solve puzzles, and follow up on clues. A treasure hunt gives your congregation a chance to do so. Working in teams, the participants will rely on clues that lead them to a series of locations in your neighborhood and ultimately back to the starting point. Give each team receives the first clue. This clue will take the teams to a location where they will get the second clue, and so on. Award one or more big prizes the first team to complete the entire course.

To create your treasure hunt, come up with eight to ten clues for the teams to follow. Determine whether the teams will stay close to the starting point and walk the course or hop in cars and drive around town. (For insurance purposes, you may need to make sure that all drivers are over a certain age. Be clear that teams should not speed to get ahead.) If you plan on sending people to any stores or restaurants, check with the management of these businesses first.

Charge each person about $5.00 to participate. Have the participants form their own teams, or assign the teams yourself. The most difficult part of organizing this event may be finding one or more big prizes to give the winning team. Try to get local vendors to donate gift certificates or merchandise for the event. They may be especially receptive to the idea if you provide free advertising by sending the teams to their establishment as a part of the treasure hunt.

Tell the teams that they may call a certain number (such as a volunteer's mobile phone number) if they are stuck and need help with a clue. Put someone in charge of answering the phone. Provide refreshments for teams who arrive first and are waiting for other teams to arrive.

VALENTINE BANQUET

Setting: On or around Valentine's Day in your church building or another location familiar to people in your congregation and community

Supplies: Food (including appetizers and punch), punch bowl, ladle, paper table cloth, napkins, dining utensils, plates, cups or glasses, Valentine-themed decorations

Major expenses: Food and decorations

Primary source of income: Admission fee

Benefit: Something for everyone to do for Valentine's Day

Having something to do on Valentine's Day is always nice, even if one isn't a romantic. An evening banquet on or around Valentine's Day can be a mid-February treat for the entire congregation. Decorate your space in red and white, with a touch of pink. Use balloons, crepe paper, construction-paper hearts, and other holiday decor to create a mood fit for Valentine's Day. Cover the tables with red paper and use white napkins as accents (or vice versa). Place red and white candles on each table. Also set aside one table for punch and either relishes and dip or cheese and crackers. Early arrivers will appreciate having something to drink and munch on as they greet and chat with one another.

Invite a DJ or live musician or band to play popular love songs, classical music, or jazz in the background throughout the night. You might have a harpist, guitarist, pianist, or strolling violinist serenade the guests.

Begin the meal with a salad, followed by a plate of spaghetti and piece of French bread. Finish it off with vanilla ice cream and heart-shaped cookies. (See the CD-ROM for recipes.) Have the youth serve dishes and clear tables.

Take reservations before and after worship on Sundays leading up to the dinner, so that you can buy the right amount of food. Spend enough money on food to ensure that your meal is complete and tasty. Charge enough to cover your costs and make a profit.

WEBSITE DONATIONS

Setting: Cyberspace, anytime

Supplies: A website and the technology to collect donations online

Major expenses: None

Supplies: Donations

Benefits: Low maintenance (after the setup)

No matter how many creative fundraisers a congregation does in the course of a year, chances are that much of the church's operating revenue still comes in through the offering plate. In addition to weekly tithes and offerings, many congregations rely on special offerings (placed in special envelopes or left at the Communion rail) to fund certain programs and mission efforts.

These days, church-offering collection isn't limited to bronze plates or wicker baskets that are passed around in the middle of the worship service. Many congregations now give members a chance to give electronically through the Internet. Often such technology is used for weekly or monthly pledges, and a set amount is automatically withdrawn from a donor's account and transferred to the church each week or month. But e-giving can also be used for special offerings, such as raising money for your next mission trip.

If your church's website already provides a means for people to donate online, check with your church's webmaster and finance committee about allowing people to donate money directly to your ministry. If you don't already have such technology, open an account with a web service such as PayPal, ParishPay (designed specifically for churches), or the *Amazon.com* Honor System, which offer a secure way to collect donations through your church or youth group website. Of course, get the approval of your church's finance committee or administrative council. Keep a record of all donations, and let the donors know (if your congregation qualifies for nonprofit, tax-exempt status) that their contributions are tax deductible.

Web donations are not likely to generate as much money as dinners or flower sales, and you probably shouldn't rely on these donations as your ministry's primary source of income. Still, this technology allows members of your congregation to give directly to the youth ministry and specific mission efforts.

WRAPPING SERVICE

Setting: In your church building on big shopping days before Christmas

Supplies: Wrapping supplies, refreshments (optional), cash box and change

Personnel needed: People who can assist the youth with wrapping

Major expenses: Wrapping supplies

Primary source of income: Wrapping charges; refreshment sales and babysitting fees (if you provide these services)

Benefits: Help for busy shoppers, reason for them to drop by the church

Offer to wrap gifts for Christmas shoppers in your congregation or community. Pick up an assortment of wrapping paper, clear tape, gift labels, pens, and accessories such as ribbons and bows from a local paper or party-supply store or a wholesale retailer. Have the youth (along with parents, adult church members, and anyone else who's willing to help out) sign up to wrap packages for busy shoppers on afternoons and Saturdays during the weeks leading up to Christmas. Set up a wrapping station in your church building. Let your congregation and community know that your group will be wrapping gifts at certain times during the Christmas season.

Consider the size of the packages, the cost of paper and supplies, and prices charged for wrapping a local stores when determining what you'll charge. Be up-front about your fee. On the busiest days before Christmas, consider selling baked goods, coffee, and hot chocolate (or providing some of these for free) to people who are waiting for their packages to be wrapped. Consider providing a baby-sitting service during the hours of wrapping, so that the shoppers can get some kid-free, efficient Christmas shopping done.

Your success—especially if the fundraiser happens every year—depends on the quality and efficiency of your work. So have the youth practice wrapping some packages before you open shop, and have people on hand who can assist youth who need to hone their wrapping skills. If you do the job well, your wrapping service could be in demand every December.

Option: Rent out a space in or near a local shopping center, and set up your wrapping station there. Some malls won't want you to compete with the wrapping services provided by stores or the shopping center itself, but others will be glad to assist a good cause and provide a service to their customers.

Ready to Go →

Cokesbury Specialty Imprints: Wear the Faith, Share the Faith

Disclosure: Cokesbury Specialty Imprints is operated by the same company that operates Abingdon Press, the publisher of this book.

Cokesbury Specialty Imprints (CSI) provides custom-made clothing and other items for churches. CSI's "Wear the Faith—Share the Faith" program offers your youth ministry a hassle-free, ready-to-go fundraiser opportunity.

The "Wear the Faith—Share the Faith" program allows you to sell eight types of shirts, all of which are printed with the name of your church and your denominational logo. (Shirt types, sizes, and colors are listed below.) Because the shirts are made to order, you won't have to worry about keeping inventory and ordering more shirts than you can sell.

If you are interested in this program, the first step is to request a free fundraiser sales packet. This packet includes

➔ full-color order forms for every person who will be taking orders. (These forms feature clear instructions and size charts for men, women, and youth.)

➔ two full-color promotional posters that feature pictures of each type of shirt offered and provide samples of the colors that are available

➔ a twelve-page manual that includes instructions, ideas, and suggestions for your fundraiser; frequently asked questions about the "Wear the Faith—Share the Faith" program; a planning calendar and goal-setting chart; and accounting and tally forms.

In addition to receiving the free packet, you can display what the shirts look like by purchasing a sample clothing kit. Each kit includes eight shirts at greatly reduced prices. The shirts come in different colors and styles and can be embroidered with your denominational logo and two lines of text.

Once you have the free packet, you can start taking orders. The members of your congregation can order any type of shirt in any size or available color. The twelve-page manual included in the packet gives information about compiling your order forms and submitting your final order.

CSI assures all customers that the products will be delivered in a timely manner.

CSI's "Wear the Faith—Share the Faith" program offers the following types of shirts:

→ **denim** (men's button down, women's straight collar): 100% cotton; choice of long sleeve or short sleeve; sizes S through XXL ($2.00 extra for XXL)

→ **adult polo:** 60/40 blend piqué; sizes S through XXL ($2.00 extra for XXL); available in white, forest green, and navy blue

→ **twill** (men's button down, women's straight collar): 100% cotton; choice of long sleeve or short sleeve; sizes S through XXL ($2.00 extra for XXL); available in white, khaki, and navy blue

→ **adult sweatshirt:** heavyweight, 90% cotton, 10% polyester; sizes S through XXL ($2.00 extra for XXL); available in white, ash, and navy blue

→ **long-sleeve T-shirt:** heavyweight, 100% cotton; sizes S through XXL ($2.00 extra for XXL); available in white, royal blue, and navy blue

→ **youth sweatshirt**: 100% cotton; sizes Youth S, M, and L; available in white and navy blue

→ **youth polo:** 100% cotton; sizes Youth S, M, and L; available in white and navy blue

→ **short-sleeve T-shirt:** 100% cotton; sizes S through XXL ($2.00 extra for XXL); available in white, royal blue, and navy blue

The following denominational logos and other symbols can be embroidered on the shirts:

➡ United Methodist (cross and flame)

➡ Presbyterian Church (U.S.A.) (cross, Scripture, dove, and flames)

➡ Disciples of Christ (chalice)

➡ Episcopal (shield)

➡ United Church of Christ (cross, crown, and orb)

➡ cross

➡ ichthus

For more information on the "Wear the Faith—Share the Faith" program and to order a sales packet, call 1-800-237-7511, go to *www.cokesbury.com/specialtyimprints,* or visit any Cokesbury store.

Safety and Sanitation

To ensure the safety of your fundraisers (particularly those involving food preparation), adhere to these rules:

- Have an adult supervisor for every five to six youth, and be sure that at least one adult supervisor is trained in first aid.
- Use warmers or oven mits when handling hot objects.
- Be careful not to burn yourself when removing dishes from the oven.
- When heating oil, keep the heat low enough so that the oil does not spatter.
- If the youth will be cutting up any ingredients, make sure that they know how to do so safely (keeping their fingers out of the way and cutting away from their fingers instead of toward them).
- Have a fire extinguisher near the kitchen.
- In case of a burn or a cut, have a first-aid kit handy. The kit should include adhesive bandages (all sizes), antibiotic cream, non-latex gloves, sterile gauze pads, adhesive tape, and scissors.
- After purchasing meat and produce, store it in the refrigerator (or the freezer, as is appropriate).
- Always wash your hands with antibacterial soap before preparing food.
- Rinse raw meat in water and pat it dry before heating it.
- Wash your hands after handling raw meat.
- Rinse produce in water before preparing it.
- Use a new spoon each time you taste a mixture.
- If your dish includes meat, produce, or both and you are not going to serve it right away, store it in the refrigerator or freezer in a closed container.
- Wash all cooking utensils after preparing food. If you've used any to prepare meat (such as a knife and cutting board), spray them with antibacterial spray.

Topical Index

FOOD

HOLIDAYS

LENT, EASTER

STUFF FOR SALE

SERVICES

YEAR-ROUND FUNDRAISERS